SECOND EDITION

Workbook

Joan Saslow • Allen Ascher

With Wendy Pratt Long

ALWAYS LEARNING

PEARSON

Summit: English for Today's World 2, Second Edition
Workbook

Copyright © 2012 by Pearson Education, Inc.
All rights reserved.

No part of this publication may be reproduced, stored in a retrieval system, or transmitted
in any form or by any means, electronic, mechanical, photocopying, recording, or otherwise,
without the prior permission of the publisher.

Pearson Education, 10 Bank Street, White Plains, NY 10606

Staff credits: The people who made up the *Summit Workbook 2* team—representing editorial, production, design,
and manufacturing— are Rhea Banker, Dave Dickey, Aliza Greenblatt, Mike Kemper, and Martin Yu.

Text composition: TSI Graphics
Text font: 10/12 Frutiger
Cover photograph: Shutterstock.com
Cover design: Elizabeth Carlson

Illustration credits: Steve Attoe: pages 13, 19, 27 (top right, bottom left) 29, 30, 58, 93, 94, 98 (top); Kenneth Batelman: page 61;
Leanne Franson: pages 52, 53; Philippe Germain: page 92; Stephen Hutchings: page 18; Suzanne Mogensen: pages 16, 41, 53, 89,
90; Sandy Nichols: page 88; Dusan Petricic: page 27 (top left, bottom right); Phil Scheuer: page 54; Steve Schulman: pages 45, 52;
Neil Stewart/NSV: pages 22, 98 (bottom), 99.

Photo credits: Page 1 (top) Alan Becker/Getty Images, (middle) Image Source Limited/Photolibrary, (bottom) Heinrich van den
Berg/Getty Images; p. 8 Cristina Quicler/AFP/Getty Images; p. 15 Nick Vedros & Assoc./Getty Images; p. 21 iStockphoto.com; p. 24
David Wasserman/Photolibrary; p. 26 (top) Bettmann/Corbis, (middle right) Mary Evans Picture Library/The Image Works, (middle
left) Gene Lester/Getty Images, (bottom) Bettmann/Corbis; p. 28 Bartomeu Amengual/Photolibrary; p. 32 Toronto Star/Zuma Press;
p. 34 Frank Trapper/Corbis; p. 37 LWA-Dann Tardif/Corbis; p. 38 (top to bottom) Banana Stock/age fotostock, Don Hammond/age
fotostock, ImageSource/age fotostock, Peter Benson; p. 44 (top to bottom) Banana Stock/age fotostock, Banana Stock/age
fotostock, Big Cheese Photo/age fotostock, Banana Stock/age fotostock; p. 46 Rainer Holz/zefa/Corbis; p. 48 Bettmann/Corbis;
p. 51 Carol Kohen/Getty Images; p. 54 Chip Simons/Getty Images; p. 56 Kevin Peterson/age fotostock; p. 64 Dave King/Dorling
Kindersley; p. 66 Victor Tonelli/Reuters/Corbis; p. 73 (top to bottom) Banana Stock/age fotostock, Banana Stock/age fotostock,
Banana Stock/age fotostock, Jacques Alexandre/age fotostock, ImageSource/ age fotostock; p. 74 (top to bottom) Bartomeu
Amengual/age fotostock, RubberBall Production/age fotostock, Jack Hollingsworth/age fotostock; p. 78 Bettmann/Corbis;
p. 79 NASA/Corbis; p. 82 (top to bottom) Art-Line Productions/age fotostock, Big Cheese Photo/age fotostock, Big Cheese
Photo/age fotostock, Medioimages/age fotostock; p. 83 DPA/SOA/The Image Works; p. 87 (A) David Davis/Photolibrary, (B) John
Lund/Getty Images, (C) Bettmann/Corbis, (D) Darwin Wiggett/Getty Images; p. 88 DPA/The Image Works; p. 89 Photodisc/Getty
Images; p. 93 Image Source/Getty Images; p. 95 (top) Royalty-Free/Corbis, (bottom) (c) The New Yorker Collection 1991 John
O'Brien from cartoonbank.com. All rights reserved; p. 103 (top to bottom) Brian Snyder/Reuters/Corbis, ITAR-TASS/Newscom,
Ausloeser/zefa/Corbis; p. 104 Bettmann/Corbis; p. 110 Toru Hanai/Reuters/Corbis; p. 115 Lynsey Addario/Corbis; p. 116 Reuters/
Corbis; p. 118 Les Stone/The Image Works; p. 120 (top to bottom) It Stock Free/age fotostock, RubberBall Production/age
fotostock, Medioimages/age fotostock, Banana Stock/age fotostock; p. 121 Mary Evans Picture Library/The Image Works;
p. 122 Xoxox Digital/Getty Images.

ISBN 13: 978-0-13-260798-8

ISBN 10: 0-13-260798-0

Printed in the United States of America

6 7 8 9 10–V001–16 15

CONTENTS

Dreams come true

TOPIC PREVIEW

1 Look at the contents page of a magazine. Then answer the questions and circle the supporting information on the magazine's contents page.

WORLD Geographer

FEATURES

27 Dog Days: Extreme winter dog-sledding adventures
Come along with *World Geographer* as we race on snowy wilderness trails commanding a sled pulled by a team of dogs!

36 Days of Darkness
There are places in the Arctic Circle where the sun doesn't rise for 67 days in the winter. Read what it's like to live without sun for over three months.

53 Due North!
A new kind of vacation— Here's an agency specializing in trips to the North Pole. See what they offer and find out how to make your reservations.

64 "I'm living my dream, and I'm getting paid to do it!"
Today it seems that more and more people are turning their hobbies into their careers. *World Geographer* talks to three people who have done it. Find out how— and learn how you can, too.

84 Dressing for the Cold
It's hard to enjoy winter activities when you're freezing cold. *World Geographer* has some hot tips to help keep you warm this season.

88 Erik Weinhenmayer: The first blind person to reach the top of Mt. Everest
He dreamed of doing it, and he turned his dream into a reality. How did he do it? What's he doing now? Interviewer Todd Gibson talks to Erik and gets this remarkable man's story.

98 STAT: Real Heroes at Work
Save the Animals Today (or STAT) is a new animal protection group with very dedicated workers. See what people give up to work there, and discover the kinds of adventures that are all in a day's work for these heroes.

1. Which article gives advice about staying warm in winter weather? ....

2. Which article might be interesting to people who enjoy exciting sports? ....

3. Which article might be interesting to people who like to travel? ....

4. Which articles probably tell about a person's goals in life? ....

5. Which articles probably tell about people's jobs? ....

2 **Read the conversation. Answer the questions.**

Mandy: Hi, Bob. What's new?
Bob: Hey, Mandy. Well, I gave notice at the office yesterday.
Mandy: Really? But I thought you liked your job.
Bob: It's OK, but I couldn't really see myself doing it for the rest of my life. I decided it was time to try something new.
Mandy: That was a big decision. Now what?
Bob: Well, my last day at the office is next Friday. After that I'm going to start working on what I've always wanted to do: open my own business.
Mandy: Way to go! You know, I could really see you as a business owner.

1. Is Bob still working at his office job? ....

2. Did Bob choose to leave his job? ....

3. Did Bob expect to work at his office job for a long time? ....

4. Does Mandy think that Bob's career change is a good idea? ....

3 **Complete each conversation. Circle the letter.**

1. A: I'm going to open my own business.
   B: I could see you doing that. ....

   a. You'll be a great business owner.

   b. It really surprises me.

2. A: How's your job at the bank?
   B: Didn't you hear? I gave notice. ....

   a. I'm starting a new job on Monday.

   b. Now I have a better job there.

3. A: Guess what? Believe it or not, I quit my job today.
   B: Way to go! ....

   a. That's great news. You hated that job.

   b. Sorry to hear that. You loved that job.

4. A: Hey, have you heard about Scott? He got married to Marcia last month.
   B: Really? He'd been thinking about asking her for a long time. ....

   a. Do you think he's going to take the plunge?

   b. What made him decide to take the plunge?

4 **What About You?** **Answer the questions in your own way.**

1. What are some reasons to give notice at a job?

   ....

2. Have you ever considered changing your career or course of study? Why or why not?

   ....

3. What job do you see yourself doing in ten years?

   ....

5 Read each conversation. Then check all the statements that are true, according to the conversation. More than one statement can be true for each conversation.

Conversation 1

Melanie: I'm considering going back to school.
Jeremy: Really? What are you thinking of studying?
Melanie: Well, I'm not sure. A college near my house offers classes in business administration. I could take classes after work.
Jeremy: You know, you really should. A business degree could really open up a lot of opportunities for you.

- ☐ **a.** Melanie is thinking about enrolling in business classes.
- ☐ **b.** Melanie has decided on a new career in business administration.
- ☐ **c.** Melanie hasn't signed up for classes yet.
- ☐ **d.** Melanie has already been accepted into the school.

Conversation 2

Julia: I've always wanted to take up golf.
Mike: Really? So what's stopping you?
Julia: Well, money, for one. It's an expensive sport.

- ☐ **a.** Julia has wanted to quit playing golf for a long time.
- ☐ **b.** Julia has wanted to play golf for a long time.
- ☐ **c.** Mike asks why Julia stopped playing golf.
- ☐ **d.** Mike asks why Julia doesn't start playing golf.

Conversation 3

Dave: I heard you're looking for a new career.
Jen: Yeah. Actually, I'm thinking about marketing.
Dave: That would be a big change.
Jen: I know. Frankly, changing jobs is a little scary.
Dave: Well, if you ask me, you should go for it. Life is short!

- ☐ **a.** Jen is a little afraid of changing her career.
- ☐ **b.** Jen is not afraid of trying a new career.
- ☐ **c.** Dave thinks that Jen should keep her old job for a few more years.
- ☐ **d.** Dave thinks that Jen should try a new career.

6 Look at the ads and messages on the bulletin board. Then use the words in the box to complete the sentences. There may be more than one correct answer.

apply for	enroll in	sign up for	take up
decide on	rejected by	switch to	

1. The Blue Dragon invites people to _____ a Tae Kwon Do club.

2. People interested in working in a hotel should call 555-3948 in order to _____ a job.

3. People interested in learning basic computer skills can _____ a computer class.

4. Carlton Test Prep might be helpful for people who've been _____ a school or program because of low test scores.

5. The ballroom dancing class is for people who want to _____ dancing.

6. People who want to _____ a different job should look at the website www.careerchange.com.

7. People who can't _____ whether to go to school or work can call 555-4545 to ask for advice.

7 Put the words and phrases in order to make correct sentences. Use the present perfect.

1. consider / you / ever / going back to school _Have you ever considered going back to school_ ?

2. ignore / never / Harry / his father's advice ....

3. the student / not / decide on / still / a career ....

4. sign up for / one course / so far / they ....

5. think about / a career in politics / never / I ....

6. recently / switch to / a new career / Jerry ....

7. medical school / already / be accepted to / she ....

8. take up / lately / you / any new hobbies .... ?

9. ask / he / her to marry him / twice ....

10. ever / they / talk about / their plans for the future .... ?

8 Challenge. Look at Abby and John's list of things to do this year. A ✔ means that the activity is done. Write sentences about Abby and John's activities. Use verbs in the present perfect and the words in the box.

To-Do List

Task	Who will do it?	Done?
buy a computer	Abby and John	
sign up for cooking lessons	John	
travel to Montreal	Abby and John	✓
apply for a new job	Abby	✓
get a pet	Abby and John	✓ (yesterday!)
go to visit her parents	Abby	✓
plant a flower garden	Abby	
enroll in a Spanish class	John	
travel to Mexico City	Abby and John	✓
take up golf	John	✓

already	just	lately	once	recently	so far	still	twice	yet

Abby has done six things on their list so far.

Abby and John have not bought a new computer yet.

....

....

....

....

....

9 What About You? Answer the questions in your own way.

1. What is something that you've done recently?

....

2. What is something that you've never done?

....

3. What is something that you haven't done yet but that you're planning to do?

....

LESSON 2

10 Read the e-mail. Underline the verbs in the present perfect. Circle the verbs in the present perfect continuous.

Dear Mom and Dad,

Well, I've arrived safely, and I'm in my hotel room in Torino, Italy. I still can't believe I'm here. My dream is finally about to come true! I'm going to skate in the winter Olympic Games! For as long as I can remember I've been dreaming of competing in the Olympics. I've worked so hard for this! I've been training for this day since you took me to my first lesson when I was four years old.

I know you and dad have given up a lot for me to be here, too. My skating lessons have been expensive, but you have never complained. Everyone has supported me. I know you will all be watching the competition on TV—you've been watching me compete since I first started skating. I hope that I do well so I can make you proud.

Your loving daughter, Tracy

11 Complete the e-mail response from Tracy's mother. Use the present perfect continuous for unfinished actions, except with stative verbs. Use the present perfect for finished actions.

Dear Tracy,

Your father and I are so proud of you! Since you were a little girl, I _have known_ that you would
(1. know)

become a great skater one day. You _____ about skating in the Olympics since we bought
(2. talk)

you your first pair of ice skates. I know that sometimes ice skating _____ like a lot of work.
(3. seem)

Injuries _____ you slow down a few times, but you _____ your goal. And now
(4. make)   (5. not forget)

your dream is finally a reality. We _____ you grow from a child to the amazing athlete and
(6. watch)

beautiful person that you are today. Over the years, we _____ you win, lose, and try again.
(7. see)

No matter what happens in Torino, we'll be proud of you just like we _____ for so many years.
(8. be)

Love always, Mom

12 **Check the sentences that are grammatically correct. Mark the incorrect sentences with an X and rewrite them, using appropriate verb forms.**

1. ☒ Since I started reading Madan Kataria's book, I've been believing in the health benefits of laughter.

   Since I started reading Madan Kataria's book, I've believed in the health benefits of laughter.

2. ☐ I've had an interest in sculpture for many years.

   ....

3. ☐ The government has considered making changes to the law.

   ....

4. ☐ My kids have been seeing that movie at least five times.

   ....

5. ☐ The group has been working on the project for over a year.

   ....

6. ☐ Since 1965, Robert De Niro has been acting in more than 75 films.

   ....

7. ☐ We've thought about moving, but we really like our neighborhood.

   ....

8. ☐ The International Red Cross has helped people all over the world.

   ....

9. ☐ I've traveled around Italy for the past few months, and I'm loving every minute of it.

   ....

13 **What About You? Complete the questions with the present perfect or present perfect continuous. Then answer the questions in your own way.**

1. What is one accomplishment that you .... (achieve) in the past?

   ....

2. What is one activity that you .... (do) for a few years?

   ....

3. What is one thing or activity that you .... (be) interested in for a long time?

   ....

4. What's one thing that you .... (love) since you were a child?

   ....

5. What's one important lesson that you .... (learn) in your life?

   ....

LESSON 3

14 **Complete the conversation. Circle the correct word in each pair.**

Nick: Did you hear I'm buying a house?

Angie: A house? When did you decide this?

Nick: Actually, it's something I've always wanted to do. It's been my (**1. lifelong / short–term**) dream to own my own home.

Angie: So now you're finally going to (**2. realize / set**) your goal. That's great! I don't think I'll ever save up enough money for a house.

Nick: You know, it's easier than you think. First you need to (**3. set / fulfill**) goals for yourself. Then you just need to (**4. take / realize**) steps to achieve them.

Angie: But houses around here are so expensive. It's discouraging!

Nick: Well, in my case, instead of worrying about my (**5. long-term / short-term**) goal of buying a house, I started small. I focused on (**6. short-term / long-term**) goals to save small amounts of money. I set goals that I could achieve in a few weeks.

Angie: Like what?

Nick: Like bringing a lunch from home instead of eating out. You'd be surprised how fast little things like that add up!

15 **Read the biography of Antonio Banderas.**

Antonio Banderas

Born in Málaga, Spain, Antonio Banderas's goal in life was clear from a young age—to become a professional soccer player. When Banderas was fourteen years old, however, he broke his foot, and the injury prevented him from playing soccer again.

While his foot was healing, Banderas attended a play at a local theater and was fascinated. In fact, after seeing that one performance, Banderas set a new goal for himself: to become an actor. He enrolled in acting school and then joined a local theater group. However, his parents disapproved of these activities. They wanted a more traditional career for their son. Nevertheless, Banderas refused to be discouraged.

For five years, Banderas traveled all over Spain with the theater group. With little financial support, the actors often performed on the street and were sometimes given a hard time by the police or by drunken audiences.

After moving to Madrid, Banderas received his first big break—an invitation to star with the country's top actors in the prestigious National Theatre of Spain. Banderas was soon noticed by Spanish writer/director Pedro Almodóvar, who asked Banderas to play a part in his comedy

Labyrinth of Passion. In the next few years, Banderas and Almodóvar made four more movies together, and Banderas began to attract attention around the world.

In 1992, Banderas acted in his first American movie, *The Mambo Kings*. At the time, the actor spoke very little English. However, determined to play an English-speaking character, Banderas signed up for intensive English lessons. He learned his lines for the movie phonetically, memorizing the sounds of the words without actually understanding many of them. Although the film was only moderately successful, critics praised Banderas's heartfelt performance.

Since that first awkward experience, Banderas has become a Hollywood star. Now more fluent in English, he has played a wide variety of characters, acting in adventure films, dramas, comedies, and family movies. Never afraid to take risks with his acting, Banderas continues to seek challenging roles.

Now read each statement. Check <u>true</u> or <u>false</u>, according to the article.

	true	false
1. Antonio Banderas has realized his dream of becoming a soccer player.	☐	☐
2. Banderas's childhood dream was to be an actor.	☐	☐
3. Banderas signed up for acting classes.	☐	☐
4. Banderas's parents supported his dream of becoming an actor.	☐	☐
5. Banderas's short-term goal when working with The National Theatre of Spain was to learn English.	☐	☐
6. Banderas took steps to achieve his goal of playing an English-speaking character.	☐	☐

16 On a separate sheet of paper, write a paragraph about Antonio Banderas's dreams and the steps he took to achieve them.

LESSON 4

17 Complete the conversation with words from the box. There may be more than one correct answer.

ability	experience	knowledge	training

Interviewer: Thank you for coming in today, Mr. Rowland. Tell me about yourself.

Mr. Rowland: I have three years' _____ working as a restaurant manager.
1.
While working at this position I've received _____ in safe food
2.
handling and preparation. I also have extensive _____ of gourmet
3.
food and wine.

Interviewer: That's great. Do you have any _____ in the travel industry?
4.

Mr. Rowland: No, I haven't actually worked in that industry. But I have the _____
5.
to plan events for large groups of people. And I've attended several seminars on
customer satisfaction, so I've had a lot of _____ in customer service.
6.

Interviewer: That's a plus. The _____ to understand customers' needs is important
7.
in this business. Another qualification that we're looking for is _____
8.
of foreign languages and culture. Can you speak any languages besides English?

Mr. Rowland: Yes. I'm fluent in French and Spanish. At my last job, I worked at a restaurant
with many foreign guests. So I have a great deal of _____ serving
9.
people from other countries.

18 A cover letter is a letter of introduction to a possible employer. It accompanies your resumé. The purpose of a cover letter is to introduce yourself and obtain an interview. Read the cover letter.

January 30, 2008

Harold Kohn, Director of Human Resources
Kate Beckham Associates
1 Park Avenue, 5th floor
Miami, FL 33132

Dear Mr. Kohn:

I am writing in response to the advertisement in *The Morning Sun*, dated January 20, for an open position for an administrative assistant. I have enclosed my resumé showing my education, experience, and background.

I have over five years of experience in the field of office management, most recently as an administrative assistant. My education includes studying in a bilingual (English-Spanish) office management program. My language abilities would be particularly useful in a bilingual office such as yours.

As my current position requires a great deal of work on the computer, I am very experienced with office software such as Word, Excel, and PowerPoint. In addition, I have taken college courses in computer graphics. Using these skills, I have been responsible for preparing sales presentations and marketing material. I have also been responsible for scheduling meetings and events for small and large groups and for organizing files and correspondence for our department.

I would like to set up an interview to further discuss my qualifications and your company's needs. I am available to meet at your earliest convenience.

Thank you for your time.

Sincerely,

Kristen Dean

Kristen Dean

Now complete the sentences about Kristen Dean using information provided in the cover letter. There may be more than one correct answer.

1. Kristen Dean has experience ....

2. She has training in ....

3. She has the ability to ....

4. She has knowledge of ....

Grammar Booster

A Read each sentence. Write **C** if the sentence is correct or **I** if it is incorrect. Fix the incorrect sentences.

1. _____I_____ I'm understanding that this is a difficult time for many employees. *I understand*

2. _____ The secretary remembers that she left the file on Mr. Johnson's desk.

3. _____ Are you having a few minutes to discuss our plans for the project?

4. _____ John is knowing your brother because they went to school together.

5. _____ I'm going to visit my travel agent today. I'm thinking of taking a vacation.

6. _____ This bag is really heavy. How much is it weighing?

7. _____ We're having steak for dinner. Would you like to join us?

8. _____ I'm believing that it's important for family members to live near one another.

9. _____ Mary is looking at photographs of her wedding.

10. _____ This sauce is tasting a little too salty.

11. _____ What are you cooking? Something is smelling wonderful.

B Complete the sentences with the simple present or present continuous of the verbs in parentheses.

1. **A:** Are these photos of your grandchildren?
   B: Yes. My oldest daughter _____ (have) two sons, and she _____ (have) another one in the spring.

2. **A:** I read that the average newborn baby _____ (weigh) between three and four kilograms.
   B: How heavy is Hannah?
   A: I don't know. The nurse _____ (weigh) her now.

3. **A:** I _____ (see) Julia in the hallway. Want me to get that file from her?
   B: No, don't bother. I _____ (see) her after lunch. We have a meeting at two o'clock.

4. **A:** The food here is delicious. They _____ (have) a lot of great seafood dishes on the menu.
   B: I don't feel like seafood tonight. I _____ (have) a salad.

5. **A:** My parents _____ (think) I watch too much TV.
   B: Mine do, too. They _____ (think) about getting rid of our television.

6. **A:** Did Anne think this sauce _____ (taste) different?
   B: I'm not sure. She _____ (taste) it now.

7. **A:** What are you doing?
   B: I _____ (look) at a photo of my brother's new house. It _____ (look) beautiful!

C **What About You?** Answer the questions in your own way. Write complete sentences.

1. What are you having for dinner tonight?

   ....

2. What are you thinking about doing this weekend?

   ....

Writing: Write a cover letter

A **Prewriting.** **Clustering ideas.** Look at the idea cluster below. On a separate sheet of paper, create your own idea cluster about your experience, knowledge, training, and abilities. Write ideas in circles and expand each new idea.

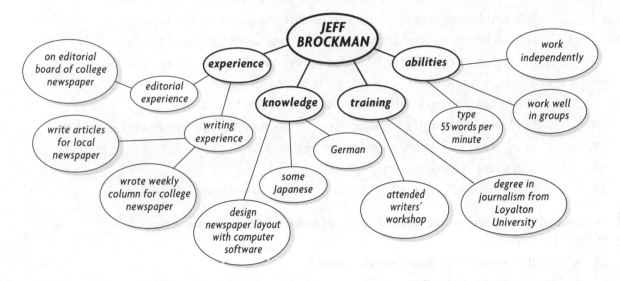

B **Writing.** Imagine that you are responding to a newspaper advertisement for a position that interests you. On a separate sheet of paper, write a cover letter. Use some of your ideas from the idea cluster. Use the cover letter in Exercise 18 as a model.

C **Self-Check.**

☐ Did you state why you are writing the letter?

☐ Did you explain why you are a good candidate for the position?

☐ Did you say what you want to happen next?

☐ Did you thank the person?

☐ Did you write any sentence fragments or run-on sentences? If so, correct them.

☐ Did you use correct punctuation?

☐ Did you use correct verb forms?

Character counts

TOPIC PREVIEW

1 Read the proverbs. Can you guess the meanings?

PROVERBS

A proverb is a short, well-known statement that gives advice or expresses something that is generally true. Proverbs often reflect the values of a culture. Here are some well-known proverbs in English. Can you guess the meanings? (Answers below.)

Ⓐ Knowledge is power.

Ⓑ Rome wasn't built in a day.

Ⓒ Opportunity only knocks once.

Ⓓ Don't count your chickens before they hatch.

Meanings: **A.** The more you know, the more information you have to help you get what you want. **B.** All large tasks take time to finish. **C.** If you get a chance to do something you really want to do, you should do it, because you may not get the opportunity again. **D.** Don't depend on anything before it actually happens.

2 Read the situations. Write the letter of the proverb from Exercise 1 that is the best match for each situation.

1. .... You've heard a rumor that your company is going to give everyone in your office a big salary increase this year. Although you can't confirm that this information is true, one of your co-workers wants to go to an expensive restaurant to celebrate. You want to prepare your co-worker for the possibility that the rumor isn't true.

2. .... A friend has been taking skiing lessons for several years. However, she still can't ski very well, and she feels frustrated by her lack of improvement. You want to advise her to remember that learning to ski requires a lot of time and practice.

3. .... Your neighbor's son has a chance to travel to another country to play in an international basketball tournament. Your neighbor thinks this would be a valuable experience, but she's anxious about the cost of the trip. You want to recommend that she allow her son to go, because he may never get another chance to do something like this.

4. .... A member of your family wants to quit high school and find a job. He doesn't think that the things he is learning will be useful to him in life, and he is eager to begin earning money and become independent. You want to suggest that the boy stay in school, because without a good education, it's difficult to succeed in life.

3 Complete each statement. Circle the letter.

1. When someone is in a bind, the person is ....
   a. forced to tell a lie
   b. in a difficult situation
   c. defending his or her character

2. A pushover ....
   a. doesn't often help people
   b. always says "no"
   c. is easy to persuade

3. When a person goes overboard, he or she ....
   a. does something that is too extreme
   b. doesn't say what he or she is thinking
   c. gets angry

4. If a person is in hot water, then he or she ....
   a. knows the truth about a situation
   b. has a big problem
   c. is acting very serious

5. If someone says "I owe you one," then he or she ....
   a. gave you money
   b. expects to help you in the future
   c. wants you to help them

4 What About You? Answer the questions in your own way.

1. Do you think that you're a pushover? Why or why not?

....

....

2. Describe a time when you were in hot water. What happened?

....

....

LESSON 1

5 Read the article. Then read each statement and check <u>true</u> or <u>false</u>.

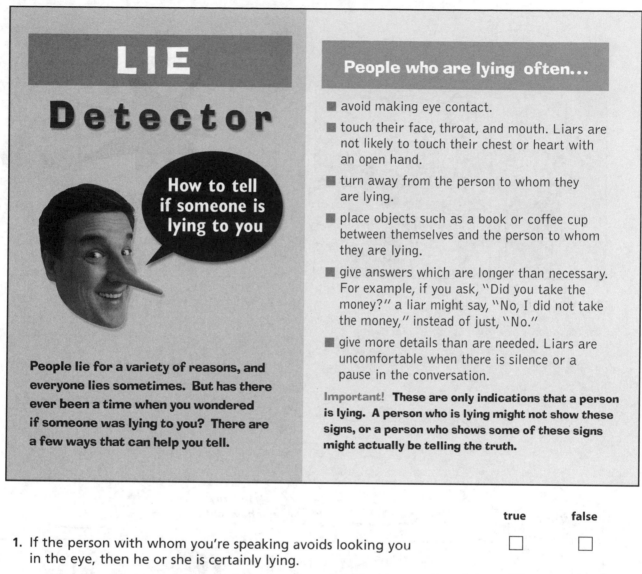

LIE Detector

How to tell if someone is lying to you

People lie for a variety of reasons, and everyone lies sometimes. But has there ever been a time when you wondered if someone was lying to you? There are a few ways that can help you tell.

People who are lying often...

- avoid making eye contact.
- touch their face, throat, and mouth. Liars are not likely to touch their chest or heart with an open hand.
- turn away from the person to whom they are lying.
- place objects such as a book or coffee cup between themselves and the person to whom they are lying.
- give answers which are longer than necessary. For example, if you ask, "Did you take the money?" a liar might say, "No, I did not take the money," instead of just, "No."
- give more details than are needed. Liars are uncomfortable when there is silence or a pause in the conversation.

Important! These are only indications that a person is lying. A person who is lying might not show these signs, or a person who shows some of these signs might actually be telling the truth.

	true	false
1. If the person with whom you're speaking avoids looking you in the eye, then he or she is certainly lying.	☐	☐
2. When people lie, they often turn their bodies away from the person to whom they are speaking.	☐	☐
3. When a person tells a lie to make an excuse, he or she might talk more than is necessary.	☐	☐
4. If a person touches his or her chest while talking, then you can be sure he or she is lying.	☐	☐

> *A person who lies for you will lie against you.*
> — Bosnian proverb

6 **Challenge. Look at the pictures. Complete each conversation by creating a lie for the second speaker. Then answer each question. Decide whether the person is lying to avoid hurting someone else's feelings or to make an excuse.**

1. Why is the girl lying?

She's making an excuse to avoid being

punished by her mother.

2. Why is the worker lying?

3. Why is the boy lying?

4. Why is the woman lying?

7 **What About You?** What would you say in each situation? Would you lie? Explain your answers.

Situation	Your response
You go to a friend's house for dinner, and he serves fish. He says, "I hope you like seafood." You hate it.	
A co-worker is wearing a new outfit. She asks if you like it. You think it's inappropriate for the office.	
A neighbor who you don't really like invites you to a party. You don't have any plans for that evening but you don't want to go.	
You forgot to do your homework. Your teacher asks why you didn't complete the assignment.	

8 **Complete the statements with <u>who</u>, <u>whose</u>, <u>whom</u>, <u>which</u>, <u>where</u>, or <u>when</u>.**

1. A liar is someone .... doesn't tell the truth.

2. There are very few people, if any, ... never lie.

3. Most people feel at least a little bit uncomfortable .... they lie.

4. Is there anyone to .... most people never lie?

5. There are times .... telling a lie can keep you out of trouble.

6. People .... lie a lot are often people .... reputations aren't very good.

7. Lying is a situation in .... most people find themselves at some point.

8. Work is one place .... people sometimes lie to avoid getting in trouble.

9 **What About You?** Complete the statements with your own words and <u>who</u>, <u>whose</u>, <u>whom</u>, <u>that</u>, <u>where</u>, or <u>when</u>.

1. .... is a person .... I'd like to meet.

2. .... is the city .... I was born.

3. .... is a holiday .... many families get together.

4. .... and .... are things .... interest me.

5. .... is someone .... ideas I find interesting.

6. .... is a person with .... I enjoy spending time.

LESSON 2

10 Look at the picture. Then write a statement describing the attitude or action of each child. Use the words in the box. There may be more than one correct answer.

admit making a mistake	make up an excuse	shift the blame to
avoid taking responsibility for	make up for	take responsibility for
express regret		

1. (Charlie) ....

2. (Sally) ....

3. (Billy) ....

4. (Jane) ....

5. (John) ....

11 Read the letter to an advice columnist. Then read the columnist's response.

Dear Anita,

I have a friend who frequently asks to borrow things from me. Since she's one of my best friends, I always say yes. But she doesn't take good care of my things. Last month I lent her a book and when she gave it back, the pages were ripped. When I asked her about it, she claimed that the pages were ripped when I loaned it to her. But that wasn't true—it was a brand new book! Another time I let her use one of my favorite handbags. I don't know how, but she got a hole in it. That time she said she was sorry, and she admitted that it was her fault, but she still hasn't given me any money for it. Once she borrowed a pair of my shoes, and her dog chewed them. But she said it wasn't her fault—it was her sister's fault because her sister let the dog into her bedroom!

I want to keep my friend, but I can't continue with the way things are going.

Please help!
Christina

Dear Christina,

You sound like a very good and forgiving friend. But it also sounds like you might be a pushover. I know it can be hard to talk openly about a friend's behavior when it bothers you. But it's important. You need to learn to say no, and your friend needs to learn to take responsibility. Next time, before you lend your friend something, tell her that you want it back in the same condition. Tell her if she doesn't return it to you the same way, you'll expect her to take responsibility for the damage. That way, you explain your expectations and make a plan if she doesn't meet them. Good luck!

Sincerely,
Anita

Now complete each statement. Circle the letter.

1. Christina's friend doesn't often ....
   a. borrow things from Christina
   b. ruin things
   c. make up for her mistakes

2. Christina's friend .... the ripped pages in the book.
   a. felt awful about
   b. made an excuse about
   c. took responsibility for

3. When Christina's friend damaged the handbag, she ....
   a. made up an excuse
   b. admitted making a mistake
   c. shifted the blame to someone else

4. Christina's friend didn't ....
   a. make up for the damaged bag
   b. know about the problem with the bag
   c. admit that the hole in the bag was her fault

5. When the dog ruined Christina's shoes, her friend ....
   a. shifted the blame to someone else
   b. took responsibility
   c. made up for the mistake

6. Anita thinks that Christina should ....
   a. express regret
   b. make excuses for her friend
   c. make her friend take responsibility

12 What About You? Read the following situation. If you were involved in this situation, would you take responsibility for the accident, avoid responsibility, or shift the blame to someone else? On a separate sheet of paper, explain your answer.

You're a college student and, to earn money for school, you have started working a part-time job at a restaurant. On your first day on the job, the manager gives you the keys to the delivery van and asks you to pick up some cakes from a bakery down the street. You have never driven a large van before but, because it's your first day, you are afraid of saying no to your new boss. When driving the van to pick up the cakes, you notice a large, luxury car parked on the street. The car has been parked too far from the sidewalk and sticks out into the street. When you pass the parked car, you accidentally hit it. You stop the van and check the damage, and you notice that the side mirror of the parked car is broken, but that the van has only a few paint scrapes. The street is empty and nobody saw the accident.

LESSON 3

13 **Read the conversations. Then describe how the people showed compassion or admiration. Use words from the box to write complete sentences.**

avoid taking responsibility	find something rewarding	look up to
be proud of	give moral support	make an excuse
do a favor	have compassion for	tell a lie

1. **Todd:** I'm really nervous about the job interview that I have tomorrow.
   Cindy: I understand, but you'll do great! You're perfect for the job.

   (Cindy) *Cindy gave Todd moral support.*

2. **Kara:** Did you know that my older sister volunteers at an animal shelter on weekends?
   Rachel: No, I didn't. That's cool.
   Kara: Yeah, I really admire her for doing it.

   (Kara) _____

3. **Mike:** I don't understand these instructions. Can you look at them please?
   Jason: Sure. I have a few minutes.

   (Jason) _____

4. **Carol:** I read in the paper about a class that is collecting money to help the poor.
   Andy: Yeah, I heard about that, too. They've collected a lot of money so far, and their teacher is really happy with their efforts.

   (The teacher) _____

5. **Jerry:** What happened to that DVD I lent you last week? It won't play anymore.
   Fred: I know. But it wasn't my fault. My baby brother was playing with it and it got scratched.

   (Fred) _____

6. **Jackie:** So how do you like your new job at the hospital?
   Sally: I love it. I have so much sympathy for people when they're sick, and it feels good to help them.

   (Sally) _____

> " A kind and compassionate act is often its own reward.
>
> — William John Bennett, U. S. politician "

14 Read the article. Then complete each statement, according to the information. Circle the letter.

AN EVERYDAY HERO

Every 56 days, Chip Brady helps save someone's life.

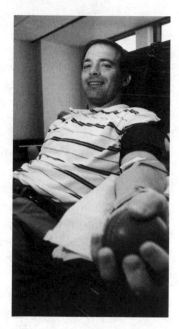

It's not anyone that he knows, and in fact he's probably never even met any of the people he's helped. Chip is a voluntary blood donor. For him, giving blood is a deep, purposeful ritual. It's a chance to express his thankfulness for his own good health, and it's an opportunity to help people in his community. "This is one way that I can truly make a difference in people's lives," he says.

It started when Chip signed up for his company's annual blood drive. He was surprised at how quick and easy the donation was. He also recalls a great sense of contentment and pride at being able to help others. He always knew that giving blood was important, but he didn't expect how great it would make him feel. "Every time I give," he says, "I get this incredible sense of satisfaction because I know that I'm helping someone in the most important way that I can. You never know who might be alive today because of your blood."

Chip admits that sometimes he gets curious about who he's helped. But in the end, he says that he has to be content with just knowing that he's done something good. Chip encourages everyone who can to donate. He wants them to know the joy that comes from helping someone in need.

1. Chip Brady likes to ....
   a. help people out
   b. feel sorry for people
   c. look up to people

2. Brady feels .... people who need blood.
   a. compassion for
   b. proud of
   c. like rewarding

3. Brady is a man who ....
   a. gives moral support to blood donors
   b. finds giving blood very rewarding
   c. feels sorry for blood donors

4. Brady's family probably ....
   a. feels proud of him
   b. finds him rewarding
   c. takes responsibility for his generosity

15 What About You? Answer the questions in your own way.

1. Have you ever helped out a stranger? How?

....

2. How do you feel when you help someone?

....

LESSON 4

16 **Read the story. Then answer the questions.**

THE ROSE AND THE CACTUS

One spring day, a red rose bloomed in a lush forest. A tall pine tree looked down at the rose and sighed. "I wish I were that beautiful." A neighboring pine tree answered, "Beauty isn't everything, you know. You give cool shade. You should be happy with that."

The rose, overhearing the pine trees, said, "I suppose I am the most beautiful plant in the whole forest." Then a sunflower turned to face the rose. "Why do you say that?" it asked. "This forest is full of beautiful plants."

"Everyone admires me," the rose answered haughtily. "And what plant is more beautiful? That ugly thing with thorns?" The rose laughed, sneering toward a nearby cactus.

Then the pine tree pointed out to the rose, "You too have thorns, you know. Does that make you any less beautiful?"

The rose snorted. "You obviously can't recognize true beauty." After that, the rose viewed the cactus with disgust. The rose said rude things and made nasty comments about the cactus. But the cactus never showed any emotion, choosing instead to reply, "Everything has its purpose."

Spring turned into summer and it grew very hot. There was no rain for long stretches and the rose began to wilt. One day the rose saw a sparrow stick its beak into the cactus. Then it flew away, appearing happy and refreshed. The rose was confused until the pine tree explained that the sparrow had been getting water from the cactus. "You can

drink from it, too," the Pine Tree said to the rose. "The sparrow can bring you water. But you have to ask the cactus for help."

The rose felt very ashamed. It finally found the courage to ask the cactus for help, and to its delight the cactus readily agreed to share its water. The sparrow filled its beak and watered the rose.

"Now I understand," the rose said softly. "I've learned a valuable lesson."

SOURCE: Traditional Arabic fable

1. What is the moral of this story?

2. Can you think of any other stories with the same or similar moral? What are they?

17 **Complete each statement. Circle the letter.**

1. At the beginning of the story, the rose ....
   a. lied to avoid punishment
   b. avoided responsibility
   c. felt proud

2. A thorn is ....
   a. a hard, sharp point that grows on the stem of a plant
   b. the part of a plant that grows underground and gets water from the soil
   c. one of the colored parts of a flower that is shaped like a leaf

3. A sparrow is _____.
   a. a kind of flower
   b. a variety of tree
   c. a type of bird

4. The rose wanted the cactus to _____.
   a. do it a favor
   b. take responsibility
   c. feel sorry for it

5. The cactus _____ the rose.
   a. gave moral support to
   b. looked up to
   c. helped out

6. Because of the cactus's generosity, the rose _____.
   a. taught it a lesson
   b. learned something
   c. shared a moral with it

18 **What About You?** Think of some children's stories that are popular in your country. What are some values that these stories teach?

Story	Value
The Ant and the Grasshopper	preparing for the future, hard work

Grammar Booster

A Read each sentence. Write **C** if the sentence is correct or **I** if it is incorrect. Fix the incorrect sentences.

1. __C__ The woman with whom I spoke was very helpful.

2. _____ The company for whom I worked was very generous.

3. _____ Now's the time when the truth comes out.

4. _____ Shirley is a girl that I've known all my life.

5. _____ The First Avenue Market is one place which I've always gotten fresh fish.

6. _____ Her ideas are ones what aren't very common.

7. _____ Is that the teacher which all the students have been talking about?

8. _____ The palace, whose history can be traced over 500 years, is a historical landmark.

9. _____ The author who stories won the contest was previously unknown.

B Complete the sentences. Circle the correct phrase in each pair.

1. The band has four members, **all of whom** / **both of whom** were born in Melbourne.

2. The guest brought a beautiful cake to dinner, **half of which** / **some of whom** was later enjoyed for dessert.

3. There are several rumors going around now, **a little of which** / **none of which** are true.

4. The artist is Alice Flannigan, **most of whom** / **one of whose** favorite colors is blue.

5. The concert includes the compositions of several local musicians, **a little of whom** / **a few of whom** have gone on to record their own albums.

6. I've heard two versions of the story, **none of which** / **neither of which** is very believable in my opinion.

C Rewrite each sentence. Reduce the adjective clauses to adjective phrases.

1. Harry Goldman works for a large company that is located in Osaka.

   Harry Goldman works for a large company located in Osaka.

2. *The Lion, the Witch, and the Wardrobe*, which is a story enjoyed by both children and adults, was written by C. S. Lewis in 1950.

   ....

3. Those photos, which prove the innocence of the defendant, have been turned over to the police.

   ....

4. People who smoke inside the building may be fined.

   ....

5. Guadeloupe, which is an island territory of France, is located in the Caribbean Sea.

   ....

6. Any student who breaks school rules will be punished.

   ....

7. The file that holds all the documentation of the study was accidentally misplaced.

   ....

Some cacti can hold up to a ton (907 kg) of water—enough to last them for two years.

Writing: Describe an experience in your life that you regret

A **Prewriting. Using Wh–questions to generate ideas.** Think about an incident in your life that you regret. Then write questions about the incident to help generate ideas.

Who ....

What ....

When ....

Where ....

Why ....

How ....

Answer your questions on a separate sheet of paper. Read what you wrote and add other ideas.

B **Writing.** On a separate sheet of paper, describe the experience that you regret, using the answers to your questions. Include details, using adjective clauses when possible.

C **Self-Check.**

☐ Did you include adjective clauses?

☐ Did you set off non-restrictive adjective clauses with commas?

☐ Using adjective clauses, can you add any more details?

WRITING MODEL

When I was sixteen years old, I had a part-time job at an ice cream store. I always worked on weekends. If I wanted to make plans to do something with friends, I had to request time off from work in advance.

One week a band that was one of my favorites was coming to town for a concert. My friends and I bought tickets. We couldn't wait! I requested the night off from work weeks ahead of time. I wanted to be sure that the plans were set.

Then, on the day of the concert I got a call from another girl, Shelly, who worked at the store. She was older than me, and she'd worked there longer than I had. She said a guy who she really liked had asked her out that night, but she was supposed to work. She asked me to go in for her. I said I couldn't because I was going to the concert. She'd have to work or figure something else out.

A little while later my boss called. He said that Shelly was really sick and she couldn't work that night. He asked me to go in instead. I couldn't believe it! She was lying to our boss! I told my boss that I had plans and couldn't do it, but he said that he really needed me and that he was counting on me. I caved in. I went in to work that night, and I missed the concert.

That was a decision which I've always regretted.

Dealing with adversity

TOPIC PREVIEW

1 Read the facts about people who overcame difficult situations.

Thomas Edison is famous for his many inventions, most notably his perfection of the electric lightbulb. Less well-known is the fact that his success with the lightbulb came only after he persisted through an estimated 10,000 failed experiments and unworkable ideas.

Built to commemorate the 100th anniversary of the French Revolution, the Eiffel Tower has become one of the most recognized symbols of France. But designer Alexandre Eiffel's masterpiece was hated by most Parisians as it was being built. It inspired such slurs as "the iron skeleton" and "the hollow candlestick."

One of the most beloved children's book authors of all time, Dr. Seuss wrote and illustrated 46 books, which have sold over 200 million copies around the world. However, his first book, the classic *And to Think That I Saw It on Mulberry Street*, was considered so unlikely to appeal to children that it was rejected by 26 publishers before one finally accepted it.

Peter Tchaikovsky is considered one of the most talented composers of all time. Yet he was not always regarded as a genius. Much to Tchaikovsky's horror, several violinists refused to play his newly written *Violin Concerto*, describing it as "unviolinistic." An influential critic of the time rejected the work as "music that stinks to the ear."

Now answer the questions in your own way.

1. Which of the facts on page 26 do you think is the most interesting or inspiring? Why?

....

....

2. What are some difficult situations that you have experienced in your own life?

....

....

2 Look at the pictures. Then check the sentence that matches each one.

1. ☐ She was going out of her mind, but he was scared to death.

   ☐ She kept her cool, but he felt a little shaky.

2. ☐ It was pitch black, but everyone kept their cool.

   ☐ When the people saw the cliff, they went out of their minds.

3. ☐ It wasn't pitch black, but it was pretty dark.

   ☐ It was pitch black, and he was going out of his mind.

4. ☐ The doctor was a little shaky.

   ☐ The patient was scared to death.

Did you know . . . that it's possible to literally be scared to death? The actual cause of death is a heart attack brought on by sudden, intense stress. And although there are hundreds of documented cases of people actually dying of fright, the statistics aren't as impressive as they might at first seem. Eighty-five to ninety percent of victims had heart disease, and their already weak hearts were pushed beyond their limits by the emotional jolt of fear.

3 Read the true story about a dangerous and challenging experience. Notice the underlined verbs.

The Brooklyn Bridge: A Story of Triumph

Already an accomplished bridge designer in the mid 1800s, John Roebling <u>wanted</u> to pursue his greatest challenge yet: building a bridge connecting Manhattan with rapidly growing Brooklyn. However, this would be no ordinary bridge. It would span the East River, which flows in more than one direction and can be navigated by ships. The bridge would have to be tall enough for ships to pass under. Roebling's idea was not well received. No one <u>had done</u> anything like it, and experts claimed it was impossible. Many people even doubted the necessity of the bridge.

But Roebling persevered, and he drew up plans for the longest suspension bridge in the world at that time. In 1869 construction began. Roebling <u>had been working</u> on the construction site for only a month when his foot was crushed in a tragic accident. Weeks later he died of complications from the injury. John's son Washington, also an engineer, <u>took over</u>.

Another tragedy soon emphasized the hazards of the project. One stage of construction <u>required</u> workers to go below the river. The effects of the changes in air pressure going from under the river to the surface killed several men and left Washington Roebling paralyzed and unable to speak. But Washington <u>wasn't giving up</u>. He could move one of his fingers a little. He slowly developed a code of communication with his wife Emily by tapping his finger on her arm. With her remarkable assistance, Washington continued to direct the project from his home. Emily took up studies in engineering to better understand Washington's plans. For thirteen years she <u>oversaw</u> work at the construction site.

Even before its opening on May 24, 1883, the bridge <u>had come</u> to symbolize triumph and ingenuity. Today the Brooklyn Bridge remains a tribute to perseverance and determination.

The Brooklyn Bridge connects the boroughs of Manhattan and Brooklyn in New York City.

Now complete the chart. Write the underlined verbs in the correct categories.

Simple past verbs	Past perfect verbs	Past continuous verbs	Past perfect continuous verbs
wanted			

4 **Complete the sentences. Use the correct form of each verb in parentheses.**

1. John Roebling _____ (try) to convince people of his plans
   past perfect continuous

   for the bridge long before the project _____ (become) a reality.
   simple past

2. John _____ (die) before his son Washington _____
   past perfect   simple past

   (take over) as chief engineer.

3. Construction of the bridge _____ (lead) to tragedies and
   simple past

   triumph in the Roebling family.

4. Emily Roebling _____ (study) engineering while her husband
   past continuous

   Washington _____ (give) orders for her to carry out.
   past continuous

5. Emily _____ (help) Washington for thirteen years before the
   past perfect continuous

   bridge _____ (be) finally complete.
   simple past

5 **Circle the action that occurred first in each sentence.**

1. (It had been raining for two weeks) when the sun finally came out.

2. He was taking a nap when suddenly the alarm clock woke him up.

3. Marianne decided to take action when she got tired of waiting.

4. By the time I found out the news, everyone had heard about it.

5. Mr. Green was waiting for a phone call when someone knocked on the door.

6. They had sent several messages to the company before they got a response.

7. Nancy had been engaged to someone else when she met Jonathan.

8. When the package finally arrived, they'd been expecting it for three weeks.

9. Jennifer saw the ad when she was looking through the newspaper.

10. I had called the office three times before I finally got hold of someone.

> "Failure is merely an opportunity to
> more intelligently begin again."
>
> — Henry Ford, 1863–1947
> U.S. industrialist,
> automobile manufacturer

6 Look at the cartoon. Then use appropriate tenses (simple past, past perfect, past continuous, or past perfect continuous) and the verbs in parentheses to complete the sentences. There may be more than one correct answer.

1. Bud _____ (consider) snowboarding down the mountain when Gretchen
   _____ (dare) him to do it.

2. Before Gretchen _____ (say) he should do it, Bud _____ (think)
   that snowboarding down the mountain was probably a bad idea.

3. Bud _____ (start) to snowboard down the mountain before Gretchen
   _____ (tell) him to stop.

4. When he _____ (hear) Gretchen yell, Bud _____ (get) really
   nervous.

5. While he _____ (roll) down the mountain, Bud _____ (decided)
   never to snowboard with Gretchen again.

LESSON 2

7 Complete the sentences with <u>no matter</u> + <u>who</u>, <u>what</u>, <u>when</u>, <u>why</u>, <u>where</u>, or <u>how</u>.

1. My grandmother hated to be told she couldn't do something.
   No matter who tried to discourage her, she never gave up her dream
   of becoming a pilot.

2. Georgia was really frustrated with the last company she worked for. She put
   in a lot of long hours, but _____ hard she worked, her boss
   never gave her any recognition.

3. That story is completely false. .... told it to you, there's no way that there's any truth to it. It's only a rumor.

4. There's never a good time to talk to Harry about that. ....
I bring up the subject, he never wants to discuss it.

5. .... anyone tells her, she's going to do what she wants.
She's not taking anyone's advice.

6. Tracy and Jack are still trying to choose a location for their wedding.
.... they decide to have it, I'm sure everything will be gorgeous. They have such great taste.

7. Credit card companies don't care if you have a good reason for making your payment past the due date. .... you're late, they still charge you a fee.

8 **Read the conversation. Then write sentences describing how the two speakers feel encouraged or discouraged. Use correct forms of the phrases in the box.**

Marissa: Hey, what's wrong? You look really stressed out.
Annie: I am. I'm not sure if I can stay at my job much longer. My boss is really tough, and sometimes that gets to me.
Marissa: I know what you mean. My boss is the same way. And it can get to me, too.
Annie: Really?
Marissa: Of course. It's natural. Everyone feels discouraged sometimes. But you shouldn't quit your job. You're smart, and you're a really hard worker.
Annie: Do you really think so?
Marissa: Absolutely. I know so.
Annie: You know what? You're right! I'm not going to quit just because things get difficult.
Thanks. I feel so much better. You really lifted my spirits.
Marissa: Anytime. You can do it. Don't forget that!

---

cheer (someone) up) / lift (someone's) spirits

discourage (someone) from (doing something)

encourage (someone) to (do something)

feel like giving up / feel discouraged

keep at it / stick with it / refuse to give up

let (something) get to you / let (something) get you down

talk (someone) out of (something)

Sometimes Annie lets her boss get her down.

LESSON 3

9 Read the true story about confronting adversity. Then answer the questions.

Storiesthatinspire.com

File   Edit   Links   Tools   Help   Chat

Stories
that inspire

Terry Fox: The Marathon of Hope

In 1977 Terry Fox was an athletic teenager growing up near Vancouver, British Columbia. But X-rays taken after Fox felt sharp pains in his right knee revealed unthinkable results: bone cancer. Fox's right leg was amputated 15 centimeters above the knee when he was only 18.

But Fox wouldn't be discouraged. Just three weeks after his surgery, he was walking with an artificial leg. He took up sports and running again, and then fostered a new, incredible plan: to run across Canada and raise money for cancer research. He set a goal of $1 for every Canadian. In letters he sent asking for sponsorship, he said: "I'm not saying that this will initiate any kind of definitive answer or cure to cancer, but I believe in miracles. I have to." He called his run "The Marathon of Hope."

On April 12, 1980, Fox splashed his artificial leg in the Atlantic Ocean and began his coast-to-coast run. He ran 42 kilometers a day (the equivalent of a marathon!) through the provinces of Newfoundland, Quebec, and Ontario. News of Fox's journey and the money he collected grew. By the time he reached Toronto, he had attained celebrity status. Crowds lined the streets to watch him pass by, providing a flood of emotional and financial support.

But on September 1, after 143 days, adversity rose again. Cancer had appeared in Fox's lungs, forcing him to stop running. At a press conference announcing the news, he said, "I just wish people would realize that anything's possible if you try. Dreams are made if people try." Inspired by these words, people rallied to collect even more money. By February 1981, $24.17 million had been raised, equal to Canada's population at the time. But while Fox's dream was coming true, he was fighting for his life. The cancer progressed quickly. Canada and the world were devastated when Terry Fox passed away on June 28, 1981, at age 22.

That September, the first Terry Fox Run was held. Over 300,000 people participated, raising $3.5 million. Terry Fox Runs are now held in 60 countries annually, through which more than $360 million has been raised for cancer research.

ONLINE

1. What obstacles did Terry Fox face? Which did he overcome? _____

_____

2. How would you describe Fox's attitude in dealing with adversity? If you were faced with challenges like Fox's, what do you think your attitude would be? _____

_____

3. Do you know someone who has inspired people by overcoming an obstacle? What obstacle did the person overcome? _____

10 Challenge. Reread the article about Helen Keller on page 32 in the Student's Book. Compare Helen Keller and Terry Fox. How are they similar? How are they different? Complete the diagram to compare these two people.

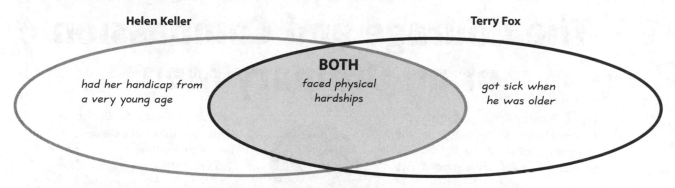

Helen Keller

had her handicap from a very young age

BOTH
faced physical hardships

Terry Fox

got sick when he was older

LESSON 4

11 Complete the chart with the correct parts of speech.

Adjective	Adverb	Noun
brave	bravely	bravery
willing		
courageous		
	heroically	
proud		
	fearlessly	
		generosity
		confidence

12 Complete the sentences. Use words from the chart in Exercise 11. There may be more than one correct answer.

1. Although Jim has studied French for many years, he lacks .... in his language ability. He never speaks in class because he's sure that he'll make a lot of mistakes.

2. The girl's parents watched .... from the audience as their daughter received her university diploma. She was the first person in the family to graduate from college.

3. Mrs. Monroe is well known for making .... donations to local charities. Last year she gave a large sum of money to the children's hospital so that they could build a new cancer treatment center.

4. The salespeople at the All-Terrain Sports Shop are always .... to help their customers. They usually offer to help before you even ask.

5. When the firefighter heard that several children were trapped in their bedrooms, he repeatedly entered the burning house to rescue them. The firefighter was honored for his ....

6. My two-year-old son isn't afraid of anything—he loves climbing, jumping, and swimming. He even loves snakes and spiders! He's completely ....

13 Read the profile of Paul Rusesabagina. Then answer the questions.

The Courage and Compassion of an Ordinary Man

Paul Rusesabagina, a manager of the Hotel Mille Collines in the Rwandan capital of Kigali, did not consider himself an extraordinary man. He was, however, an exceptionally effective businessman, skilled at using his connections with the rich and powerful to keep his hotel running smoothly and to obtain for his hotel guests the best of everything. He knew, for example, that flattering words and gifts of imported liquor and cigars would win him favors from government officials.

But on April 6, 1994, neither Rusesabagina nor most Rwandans could get the only thing that they wanted: safety. On that day, an ethnic group known as the Hutus began killing another ethnic group, the Tutsis. As a Hutu,

Paul Rusesabagina saved the lives of over 1,200 people during the Rwandan genocide of 1994.

Rusesabagina was safe. But his wife, a Tutsi, and their three children, were not. With his thoughts focused on his family, Rusesabagina took them to the hotel for safety. He didn't consider taking in other Tutsis or making the hotel a refuge. But as people arrived at the hotel begging for help, he felt he had no choice. Rusesabagina ended up accepting over 1,200 refugees into the hotel.

For 100 days while the killing went on outside, Rusesabagina held off the soldiers from invading the hotel. He used money and luxury goods from the hotel to bribe them. He called in every favor owed to him. When the killing was finally over, Rusesabagina, his family, and most of the refugees had survived.

1. Why do you think Paul Rusesabagina did not consider himself an extraordinary man?

   ....

   ....

2. According to the profile, what special talents or abilities did Rusesabagina have?

   ....

   ....

3. Do you think that Rusesabagina's experiences or actions in Rwanda made him a hero? Explain why or why not.

   ....

   ....

Grammar Booster

A Complete each sentence. Circle the letter.

1. She _____ to work when her car suddenly started smoking.
   a. would drive   b. has driven   c. was driving

2. I _____ Turkish food a few times, and I really like it.
   a. used to eat   b. have eaten   c. was going to

3. We _____ soccer last weekend.
   a. would play   b. used to play   c. played

4. They _____ vegetables at the market this morning, but it was closed.
   a. were going to buy   b. bought   c. would buy

5. I _____ you yesterday, but I didn't have time.
   a. had called   b. was going to call   c. was calling

6. Everyone _____ at the office at 8:30 this morning.
   a. was   b. used to be   c. has been

7. The workers _____ painting the house before the storm started.
   a. have finished   b. used to finish   c. had finished

8. I always knew I _____ a house near the beach one day.
   a. would buy   b. bought   c. had bought

9. Tom _____ meat, but now he doesn't.
   a. was going to eat   b. used to eat   c. was eating

B Cross out the word or phrase that does <u>not</u> correctly complete each sentence.

1. As a child, Betsy **used to bother / bothered / was bothering** her younger brothers a lot.

2. The team **had been working / used to work / had worked** on the project for months before it was finally finished.

3. I **had walked / walked / was walking** there twice before I learned I could take a bus.

4. The secretary **had left / left / was leaving** a message for Mr. Reynolds on Monday evening before she went home.

5. She thought that she **would see / had seen / had been seeing** that movie by herself.

6. She **used to study / has studied / studied** all the time when she was a student.

7. They **were waiting / had been waiting / waited** for over an hour before their table was ready.

C What About You? Answer the questions in your own way.

1. What did you do yesterday evening?

   _____

2. What is something that you used to do when you were a child?

   _____

3. What is something that you thought you would have done by the age that you are now?

   _____

4. What is something that you've done a few times in the past year?

   _____

Writing: Write a story about a hero

A **Prewriting.** "Freewriting" to generate ideas.

- Choose a story about a hero. It can be a true or fictional story. It could be about someone you know personally or someone famous. On a separate sheet of paper, write for five to ten minutes all the details about the story you can think of. Write quickly. Do not take time to correct spelling, punctuation, verb forms, time order, etc.

- Then read what you wrote. Choose ideas you would like to develop and put them in logical order.

B **Writing.** On a separate sheet of paper, tell your story. Use adverbial clauses and phrases as well as prepositional time phrases and sequencing words and phrases to narrate past events logically. Use the story about Paul Rusesabagina in Exercise 13 as a model.

C **Self-Check.**

- ☐ Is the chronological sequence of the events in your narrative clear and logical?

- ☐ Did you use time and sequence words?

- ☐ Did you use the correct punctuation?

- ☐ Did you use correct past tense verb forms?

Prepositional time phrases
on Fridays
in May
from January to May
at 8:00
by April
during that time

Sequencing words and phrases
First,
Next,
Then,
After that,
Finally

Personality and life

TOPIC PREVIEW

1 **Look at the website.**

File   Edit   Links   Tools   Help   Chat

A Better You

If you're like most people, then there are probably a few things you'd like to change or improve in your life. Check out this list of the most common resolutions that people make. Notice any of yours among them? Click on any that sound familiar for links that'll help you follow through with your good intentions.

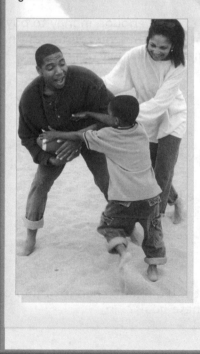

Spend more time with loved ones.

What fun is life if you don't share it with the people you care about most? If you don't have enough time for them, then you've got to *make* time. They'll appreciate it, and you'll reap the benefits, too.

Get in shape.

You'll look and feel better if you start taking care of your body. The health benefits of regular exercise are substantial, and maintaining a healthy weight is vital to reducing the risk of illness and increasing longevity.

Help others.

Whether it's teaching a child to read, volunteering in your community, or building a house, there are so many ways to make a difference in someone's life. Charitable organizations always welcome donations of time, money, and talent.

Manage your money.

Is money a big source of stress in your life? Whether you want to get out of debt, increase your savings, or just start spending more sensibly, there are lots of ways to get a handle on your finances.

Manage your time.

Not enough hours in a day to get everything done that you need to? That may be true, but you can still accomplish a lot by simply prioritizing your activities and carefully planning when and how often to do each one.

Break a habit.

Whether it's smoking, drinking too much coffee, or spending beyond your means, many of us have habits that are self-destructive. Willpower is the key to fighting habits that bring us temporary pleasure but can cause harm in the long run.

ONLINE

Now read the interviews. For each person, choose the resolution on the website that best matches the person's goal or situation.

1. "My goal? That's easy. I want to fit into the suit I wore when I got married. I tried the suit on last week and I couldn't even button the vest. I've only been married a year and a half! I think every guy thinks he's just a few sit-ups away from a flat, washboard stomach. It was a shock to see how much weight I've gained in such a short time."
   — *Kyle Senk, Toronto, Canada*

2. "I'm really fortunate that I had the opportunity to receive a good education. I know that there are lots of kids who weren't as lucky as I was, and I'd like to do something to give them a chance to learn. Maybe I could volunteer at a local school as a reading or math coach."
   — *Kavita Singh, New Delhi, India*

3. "I spent my twenties focused on getting the next big promotion, more responsibility at my job, and a higher salary. Now I look back and realize that my job was my whole life. From now on I want to spend more evenings and weekends with my family and start accepting my friends' invitations to get together." — *Carlos Costas, Lima, Peru*

4. "I make a decent salary, but I just can't save up enough money to buy my own home. Everything I earn gets spent on clothes, nice restaurant meals, movies. I wonder if I'm handling my finances as wisely as I could."
   — *Yoshiko Une, Kashiwa, Japan*

2 **What About You?** **Answer the questions in your own way.**

1. Do you think any of the resolutions on the website might be helpful to you? Why or why not?

2. Do you ever make resolutions about things in your life that you'd like to change or improve? If so, have you been successful in following through with these goals?

3 Read the situations. Then identify each problem. Write the letter on the line.

PROBLEMS		
a. disorganization	d. insomnia	g. getting angry easily
b. low self-esteem	e. inability to follow through	h. sedentary lifestyle
c. procrastination	f. poor test-taking skills	

SITUATIONS

1. .... For the past three months, you've been having difficulty sleeping. Most nights, you get only a few hours of sleep. This is causing problems at your job, as you're so tired during the day that you're finding it hard to get your work done.

2. .... After a few months at your new job, you've had minimal success. You don't feel very good about yourself, and you lack confidence in your abilities.

3. .... You start projects with excitement and energy, only to have your enthusiasm fizzle out before you're done. Your "to-do" list is filled with unfinished tasks that you've lost interest in.

4. .... Although you used to be pretty active, you find that now your lifestyle involves driving to work, sitting in front of a computer all day, then watching television in the evenings. You can't remember the last time you got some exercise.

5. .... You spend more time looking for all the things you'll need to do a project than you spend working on the project itself. Nothing is where you think you left it or where it should be.

6. .... With the due date for a big assignment quickly approaching, you just can't seem to make yourself do it. You'll do anything to avoid it, even clean the house, do the laundry, or go to the gym—activities that you normally hate.

7. .... Every little thing seems to bug you lately. Situations that don't really bother other people can make you really frustrated. Problems that annoy others make you feel angry.

8. .... You've studied for days, but as soon as you see the exam questions in front of you, your mind suddenly goes blank. You can't remember information that you know inside and out.

4 Read the conversations. Replace each phrase in parentheses with a vocabulary item from the box. Not all vocabulary items will be used.

(be) a gossip	confide in (someone)	racket
(be) out in the open	get hold of himself/herself	shame on (someone)
(be) ticked off	keep a secret	talk behind (someone's) back

Conversation 1

Kara: What's that .... (loud noise)?

Daria: That's my son, Dave. He just took up the drums.

Kara: The drums? You couldn't talk him into trying something a little quieter?

Daria: Actually, the drums were my idea.

Kara: Your idea?!

Daria: Yeah, well, he has some problems controlling his anger. We thought that whenever he .... (is annoyed) about something, he could just bang away on his drums!

Conversation 2

Pam: Hey, Scott. Do you have a few minutes?

Scott: Sure. What's up?

Pam: Well, I really need to _____ (talk to someone I can trust).

Scott: Come in. Sit down. Tell me everything.

Pam: Thanks. Do you mind if I close the door? I really don't want Penny to hear this. You know that she _____ (loves to spread rumors).

Scott: No problem. Shut the door.

Conversation 3

Russ: Hey, did you hear what Debbie did this morning?

Jessica: No. What happened?

Russ: You know she had that big meeting with Easton-Thurman? Well, they kept rejecting all her ideas and she got so mad that she had to leave the meeting to _____ (calm down).

Jessica: Wow. Maybe we shouldn't tell anyone else. I like Debbie, and I don't want to _____ (say things without her knowing).

Russ: Oh, it _____ (isn't a secret). Everyone knows about it.

Whoever gossips to you will gossip about you.
—Spanish proverb

LESSON 1

5 **What About You?** Read each statement. Use the phrases in the box to say whether it describes you or doesn't describe you. Explain your answers.

I'm just the opposite.	I'm not like that.	Not me.
I'm like that myself.	Me, too.	That's my problem, too.

1. If I don't write a "to-do" list, I forget what I need to get done.

   (YOU) _____

2. I get excited coming up with ideas for new projects, but then I lose interest.

   (YOU) _____

3. I have trouble relaxing.

   (YOU) _____

4. I wake up at night and worry about all the things I need to do the next day.

   (YOU) _____

5. I like to carefully plan my activities each day.

   (YOU) _____

6. I often give people my opinion, even if they don't ask for it.

   (YOU) _____

7. I always remember people's faces, but I'm not good at remembering names.

   (YOU) _____

6 Challenge. Read about the problem. Then read how each employee reacts.

THE PROBLEM: A group of employees is reviewing a presentation they're going to give the following afternoon. Although the presentation has some good aspects, there are problems that will take the group several hours to fix.

THE EMPLOYEES' REACTIONS:

Jane: She ignores the positive aspects of the presentation and spends the meeting pointing out all of the problems. She becomes very upset and is convinced that she will lose her job when the boss sees the presentation.

Liz: As the junior member of the group, Liz is asked to stay late to work on the project. Although fixing the project by herself will take her all night, she agrees. She feels a great deal of stress about this because she doesn't have a lot of experience in preparing presentations.

Robert: He agrees that the presentation needs some work, but he opposes the idea of working late to fix it. He suggests putting off fixing the presentation until the next morning. He reasons that everyone will work better after a good night's sleep.

Jordan: Like Jane, he is also critical of the presentation. In addition to the big problems that Jane mentioned, he points out many smaller, not-so-important details as well. When he learns that Liz will be working on the presentation, he gives her a long list of minor improvements to make.

Now write statements describing the attitude or behavior of each employee. Use expressions from the box. Predict what consequences these attitudes might have for the group members. There may be more than one correct answer.

(be) a perfectionist	(have) a negative attitude
(be) unable to say no to requests	overreact to things
take on more than (one) can handle	wait until the last minute

1. (Jane) *Jane has a negative attitude. By making herself upset, she may not be able to focus on a solution to the problem.*

2. (Liz) ....

....

3. (Robert) ....

....

4. (Jordan) ....

....

7 Take the stress quiz and calculate your results.

HOW STRESSED ARE YOU?

Take our quiz and find out!

Read each statement. How often do you find yourself exhibiting that attitude or behavior? Write the number that corresponds to your answer on the line. When you complete the quiz, add up your total number of points. Read what your score means.

4 = Always
3 = Frequently
2 = Sometimes
1 = Never

_____ **1.** You feel guilty and uncomfortable when you're just relaxing and doing nothing.

_____ **2.** You try to do more than one thing at a time.

_____ **3.** You enjoy games only if you win.

_____ **4.** You spend a lot of time away from your family and friends.

_____ **5.** You dislike asking for help when you have a problem.

_____ **6.** You look at your watch or clock more than twice in one hour.

_____ **7.** You take on so many projects that you don't have time to do any of them well.

_____ **8.** While walking on the street, you get irritated by people who walk slowly.

_____ **9.** You don't have enough time to enjoy hobbies or leisure activities.

_____ **10.** Worries about work or school prevent you from sleeping well.

_____ **YOUR SCORE (Add up all the numbers.)**

WHAT YOUR SCORE MEANS

15 and below:	You may be too relaxed. A little stress can be a good thing if it motivates you to get things done. It's important that you challenge yourself more.
16—25:	You're able to handle and control stress well. We recommend that you be aware of the sources of stress in your life and watch for rising stress levels.
26—30:	Your stress level is high. We recommend that you experiment with stress-busting techniques to help you keep your cool.
over 30:	You're completely stressed out. It's critical that you learn how to manage your stress or health problems could result.

Now answer the questions in your own way.

1. Do you agree with the results of the quiz? Why or why not?

   ....

   ....

   ....

2. Describe one situation in your life that stresses you out. Why does it cause you stress?

   ....

   ....

   ....

3. What are some specific ways that you can reduce stress in your life?

   ....

   ....

   ....

Statistics from a recent stress research study show that rising stress levels is a global problem, and that women report the greatest levels of stress worldwide.

- Women who work full-time and have children under the age of 13 report the highest stress levels.
- Nearly one in four mothers who work full-time and have children under the age of 13 feel stress almost every day.
- 23% of women executives and professionals, and 19% of their male colleagues, say they regularly feel "super-stressed."

Source: Roper Starch Worldwide survey of 30,000 people between the ages of 13 and 65 in 30 countries.

8 **Read each sentence. Write C if the sentence is correct or I if it is incorrect. Fix the incorrect sentences.**

1. __I__ A health counselor suggested that Kim reduces her stress levels.
   reduce

2. .... It is agreed that too much stress causes physical problems.

3. .... The company insists that people not smoke on company property.

4. .... I've suggested that she talk to her doctor about stress management techniques.

5. .... If you demand that your daughter doesn't keep secrets from you, she'll want to share things with you even less.

6. .... It's desirable that no one knows the details of the project before it is announced.

7. .... It's essential that each person remember his or her role in the process.

8. .... I feel it's necessary that you be aware of how your actions affect others.

LESSON 3

9 Read about the people. Then summarize the way each person handles anger. Use expressions from the box. There may be more than one correct answer.

hold it back	let off steam	say what's on (one's) mind
keep it in	lose one's temper	take it out on someone
let it go /shrug it off	make an issue out of something	tell someone off

Because Joe works as a salesperson, he has to be nice to customers all the time, even if they really make him angry. When he gets home after a bad day at work, he sometimes yells at his kids for no reason.

Beth found an effective way to control her anger. Whenever she gets mad, she leaves the office and takes a 10-minute walk. When she gets back to the office, she's usually in a much better mood and she's better able to deal with her problem.

After several weeks of being badly treated by his boss, Luis finally got ticked off and yelled at him. Surprisingly, his boss didn't fire him. He actually gave Louis a few days off and began treating him better.

Maggie feels uncomfortable displaying her emotions, so you can never really tell if she's angry. Even when people really upset her, she never lets them know how she feels. She's a closed book.

1. (Joe) ....

2. (Beth) ....

3. (Luis) ....

4. (Maggie) ....

10 **Read the story.**

There once was a woman who always bought fruit and vegetables from the same local farmer. This farmer had earned a good reputation for the freshness and tastiness of his produce, which he delivered himself in an old truck.

Then, one day, the woman planned a large dinner party. She placed a large order with the farmer to be delivered on the day of the party. However, the day of the party arrived and the farmer did not deliver the goods as promised. Without the necessary ingredients, the woman was unable to cook the wonderful meal that her guests expected. Short of food, she was embarrassed that many of her guests left her party hungry.

The next morning, the farmer appeared at the door carrying the produce that he had promised. The woman, unable to control her anger, yelled at the man, calling him irresponsible and lazy. She threatened to stop buying his products. "What do you have to say for yourself?" the woman demanded.

The farmer answered, "I'm sorry to have inconvenienced you. I didn't make your delivery yesterday because my mother passed away."

Ashamed about the way she had spoken to the man, the woman vowed never to speak in anger again.

Now summarize the lesson that the woman in the story learned about handling anger. Use expressions from the box in Exercise 9 or your own words.

....

....

....

....

11 **What About You?** **Complete the sentences in your own way.**

1. When I get ticked off, sometimes I ....

2. Sometimes I .... to let off steam.

3. I sometimes lose my temper when ....

4. Sometimes I take out my anger on ....

12 Read the article. Then read the statements and check <u>true</u> or <u>false</u>.

KINBURG TIMES-HERALD

Tuesday, March 3

Local Family Gives Up a Lot—And Has Everything to Gain

KINBURG At ages 32 and 34, Fiona and Nigel Vaughn had achieved many of their life goals: successful careers, a healthy family, a beautiful home. Although these were the things they'd always wanted, they still felt like something was missing. "I remember thinking that this can't be all there is to life," said Fiona. "There must be something more."

So the Vaughns did some real soul-searching. They asked themselves tough questions about what was really important in their lives. Nigel explained, "We have two young daughters, and we thought a lot about what we wanted to teach them."

Then Fiona found out about an organization called Care for Africa. The organization recruits dedicated people who are willing to go to Africa to work in community development projects, education, and health care. "I was interested immediately. This was a way for us to do something really meaningful with our lives."

They talked about the decision for a year to be certain that they were making the right choice for themselves and their family. "But the more we thought about it, the more we knew it was right," Nigel says.

In two weeks, the Vaughn family is moving to Kenya. They've sold their house. They've given a few items to family and friends, but they've sold most of their belongings. And they couldn't be happier.

"It'll be a huge change, and we know we won't have all the comforts we're used to. There's a good chance that we'll be living in a place without running water or electricity," Fiona explains. "But we've decided that helping others is what's really important in our lives."

	true	false
1. The Vaughns made a choice between a life they know and a new life in a new place.	☐	☐
2. Fiona didn't think it made sense to trade the comforts of her beautiful home for a house without electricity.	☐	☐
3. Fiona and Nigel made a decision to change careers because they were unhappy making do with low pay and long hours.	☐	☐
4. The Vaughns wanted to make a difference in other people's lives.	☐	☐
5. The Vaughns made sure to think about their decision for a long time before making a change.	☐	☐

13 Look at the list. How important is each of these things to you? Rate each one from 1 to 5 (5 is very important, 1 is not important at all). Then answer the questions in your own way.

.... making a lot of money

.... learning new things

.... helping others

.... relaxing each day

.... staying close with my family

.... keeping in touch with my friends

.... staying healthy

.... looking good

1. How does the amount of time that you spend on each of these activities compare to how important it is for you? Are you doing what you think is important?

....

....

2. Do you think that you make enough time in your life for things that you rated the highest? Why or why not?

....

....

14 **What About You?** Answer the questions in your own way.

1. Do you know anyone who has made a big life change? What was the change and what was the reason for it?

....

....

2. Describe a time when you had to make do with something that wasn't what you would have liked.

....

....

3. What person has made the most difference in your life? Explain your reasons for choosing this person.

....

....

"Don't ask yourself what the world needs—ask yourself what makes you come alive, and then go do that. Because what the world needs is people who have come alive."

—Harold Thurman Whitman, philosopher and theologian

Grammar Booster

A **Complete each sentence. Circle the correct word or phrase.**

1. If you have time, I suggest **stopping / to stop** for lunch at one of those restaurants.

2. The coach recommends **to get / getting** a good night's sleep before each game.

3. For the team to be successful, it's essential **to work / working** together.

4. Mr. Hammond said it's critical **getting / to get** the package to Shanghai by tomorrow morning.

5. It's urgent **to start / starting** the process today.

6. The airline suggests **to arrive / arriving** at the airport check-in counter two hours before an international flight.

B **Complete the sentences with the infinitive or gerund forms of the verbs in parentheses.**

1. Doctors recommend .... (exercise) at least three times a week.

2. It's critical that people work .... (protect) the Earth's environment.

3. I heard that it's necessary .... (arrive) at the theater two hours before the show starts if you want to get tickets.

4. She advised .... (seek) help from a local historical society.

5. The teacher suggested .... (write) an outline to help us organize our ideas.

6. It's important .... (make) a budget for your personal expenses.

C **What About You?** **Complete the sentences in your own way. Use infinitive and gerund phrases.**

1. When I was younger, people advised me ....

....

2. If a person wants to be healthy, I recommend ....

....

3. If a person wants to be successful in life, it's important ....

....

"A great victory in my life has been the ability to accept my shortcomings and those of others. I'm a long way from being the human being I'd like to be, but I've decided I'm not so bad after all."

— Audrey Hepburn, actress, model, special ambassador to the United Nations Children's Fund (UNICEF), 1929–1993

Writing: Tips for making a change

 A **Prewriting. Outlining to generate ideas.** Choose one of the changes in the box or think of your own. Write it on the line labeled "Change" and then propose three ways of making the change.

Change: ....

Ways to make the change:

1. ....

2. ....

3. ....

CHANGES:
- Overcoming a shortcoming
- Reducing stress
- Managing anger
- Adopting a new lifestyle
- Your own idea: ....

Example:

Change: *overcome perfectionism*

Ways to make the change:

1. *be less critical of myself when I make mistakes*

2. *learn to accept myself the way I am*

3. *set realistic goals*

B **Writing.** On a separate piece of paper, develop each way listed in Exercise A into a paragraph. Start all three paragraphs with topic sentences. Be sure to use a transitional topic sentence for paragraphs 2 and 3.

C **Self-Check.**

☐ Does the first paragraph have a topic sentence?

☐ Do the following paragraphs have transitional topic sentences?

Presenting contrasting information

In contrast,

Some people believe ...,

On the other hand, ...

Even though ...,

In spite of the fact that ...

Nevertheless, ...

Presenting additional information

In addition to the [ideas presented above], ...

Furthermore, ...

Moreover, ...

Besides [the information already presented], ...

It's all in your mind

TOPIC PREVIEW

1 **Read the superstitions. Guess the country where each superstition originated. Write the letter on the line. (See answers below.)**

1. .... A bride should not wear pearls on her wedding day because they represent the tears she will cry in her marriage.

2. .... The first person who visits your home in a new year will be important in your life for the rest of the year.

3. .... If you find one white hair on an all black cat, you'll have good luck.

4. .... If you stand between two people whose names are the same, make a wish: the wish will come true.

5. .... Don't wash your hair before you take a test. If you do, you'll wash away your memories and forget what you studied.

6. .... If you always put sugar in your coffee cup before you add coffee, you'll become rich.

a. Turkey

b. Vietnam

c. Argentina

d. Mexico

e. Korea

f. France

1. d. Mexico 2. b. Vietnam 3. f. France 4. a. Turkey 5. e. Korea 6. c. Argentina

2 **What About You?** **Answer the questions in your own way.**

1. What are some popular superstitions from your own country?

....

....

2. Do you believe in any of these superstitions? Do you ever follow superstitions, even if you don't believe in them? Explain why or why not.

....

....

....

....

3 Read the article. Then complete the statements, according to the article. Circle the letter.

Aisle or Window Seat? Superstitious or Non-superstitious?

In today's scientific world, many people are reluctant to admit to believing in superstitions. But talk to a few people in the travel industry, and you'll soon learn that superstition is alive and well around the world.

In much of the Western world, the number 13 is considered bad luck. Next time you're traveling by air, try looking for row number 13 on your airplane. Chances are, there isn't one. Few airlines have a row 13, and most airlines don't offer flight numbers that contain that number. The airlines offer different reasons for this. One airline spokesperson noted that the taboo associated with the number 13 is an old tradition that has persisted only because it would be too expensive to renumber the rows on hundreds of airplanes. A spokesperson for a different airline admitted that the airline omits row 13 because too many passengers refuse to sit in those seats. Travel industry studies even show that travel declines on "unlucky" days, such as the thirteenth day of the month.

In parts of Asia, the number 4 is considered unlucky because it has a similar pronunciation to that of the Chinese word for "death." In Japan, the number 9 is avoided because it sounds like the Japanese word for "torture." Some Asian airlines skip these numbers when numbering airplane rows. (Curiously, although the number 13 is not considered unlucky by most Asians, row 13 is also often skipped.) Visit Seoul's brand-new Inchon Airport, and you'll notice that there are no gates numbered 4, 13, or 44.

Superstitions about numbers can also be positive. In China, the number 8 is considered lucky because its pronunciation is similar to that of the Chinese word that means "to strike it rich." When one airline recently introduced a flight from Beijing to Newark, they named it Flight 88 and offered a "lucky" $888 round-trip ticket price. In the United States, where the numbers 7 and 11 are believed to bring good fortune, flight numbers containing these numbers are very common for flights to the gambling casinos of Las Vegas.

Superstitious behavior isn't limited to passengers—flight attendants and flight crew have a reputation for being superstitious, too. Some have been known to refuse hotel rooms whose numbers coincided with those of flights that ended in tragedy.

Whether our superstitions are rooted in tradition or personal experience, it seems that most of us pack them up and take them with us, no matter where in the world we travel.

1. The article _____.
   a. offers advice on avoiding bad luck on a trip
   b. recommends that the travel industry change policies that are based on superstitions
   c. explains how superstitions affect the travel industry

2. _____ is considered by many travelers to be unlucky.
   a. A seat in the thirteenth row of an airplane
   b. An airline flight number that contains the number 8
   c. An airport gate numbered 7

3. The article claims that _____.

    a. passengers are more superstitious than flight attendants

    b. Asian travelers are more superstitious than travelers from other parts of the world

    c. some passengers avoid traveling on days of the month that are considered unlucky

4. The article does not claim that _____.

    a. believing in superstitions is old-fashioned

    b. superstitions exist all over the world

    c. some airlines choose lucky flight numbers to increase ticket sales

4   **What About You?**   **Answer the questions in your own way.**

1. What numbers are considered lucky or unlucky in your country? Can you explain why?

_____

_____

2. Are there any numbers that you personally consider lucky or unlucky? Why or why not?

_____

_____

5   **Complete the sentences. Use phrases from the box. Not all of the phrases will be used. Some will be used more than once.**

a bolt of	a clap of	a game of	a loaf of	a symbol of	an article of
a bowl of	a drop of	a grain of	a piece of	an act of	

1. According to Chinese feng shui, Mandarin ducks are _____ love because they mate with a single partner for life. Placing a pair of wood or crystal ducks in the southwest corner of your home is said to improve your romantic life.

2. British sailors who were experiencing bad luck on an ocean voyage had an unusual method of discovering the person responsible—they baked _____ bread with _____ wood inside. At mealtime, the unfortunate sailor who found this wood in his bread was determined to be unlucky and was ordered off the ship.

3. In many Asian countries, standing chopsticks upright in _____ rice is very bad manners—it's _____ death.

4. According to one old superstition, _____ thunder after a funeral means that the person's soul has reached its final resting place.

5. Although people of some ancient cultures feared strong storms, early Scandinavians welcomed them. They believed that _____ lightning during a summer storm caused crops to ripen.

6. A common modern-day superstition, especially among athletes, is the belief that _____ clothing can bring good luck. Some athletes even refuse to wash their lucky clothing until the end of their competitive season.

7. One superstition about witches states that any witch who does harm to another person will receive three times that much harm upon herself. But _____ kindness will be rewarded threefold.

8. According to a superstition from Belize, _____ blood taken from the little finger of a man's left hand and secretly put in a woman's drink will make the woman fall passionately in love with him.

---

6 **Read the superstitions. Write C if the sentence is correct or I if it is incorrect. Fix the incorrect sentences.**

1. __I__ If you play a tennis, it's bad luck to hold more than two balls when you serve.

2. _____ Never play a game of cards with a dog in the same room, or it will lead to arguments.

3. _____ To ensure a "sweet life," a bride should put a few grains of sugar in her glove on her wedding day.

4. _____ Be careful with salt. You'll cry one tear for each salt that you spill.

5. _____ Pulling out a white hair will cause ten more to grow in its place.

6. _____ Dropping a comb while you are combing your hairs is a sign of a coming disappointment.

A Joke

One day, a little girl noticed that her mother had several white hairs sticking out from the rest of her dark hair.

The girl looked at her mother and asked, "Mom, why are some of your hairs white?"

Her mother replied, "Well, every time that you do something that worries me, one of my hairs turns white."

The little girl thought about this for a while, and then said, "Mom, how come ALL of Grandma's hairs are white?"

LESSON 2

7 Complete the sentences. Insert <u>a</u>, <u>an</u>, or <u>the</u> before a noun or noun phrase where necessary. Write *X* if the noun should not have an article.

1. Phishing is .... scam designed to steal a person's identity. Victims of .... scam receive .... e-mail that appears to come from .... trusted website such as their bank or favorite shopping site. .... e-mail attempts to trick people into disclosing valuable personal information like credit card numbers, passwords, or account data.

2. Until the 1800s, British doctors believed that .... tomatoes were poisonous and caused conditions like "brain fever" and cancer. In fact, ... tomato is highly nutritious and a good source of vitamin A, important for healthy hair and skin.

3. There's .... new product being marketed on .... Internet called "Exercise in a Bottle." In pop-up ads, the company claims that .... product will burn fat while the user is just sitting around doing nothing or even sleeping. .... ads also state that consumers can enjoy fried chicken, pizza, and other high-calorie, high-fat products and still lose weight.

4. .... U.S.-based company is in the business of selling stars. For $48 you can purchase .... star and name it. .... company has faced a great deal of criticism from .... astrologers and consumer groups, who point out that the certificates of purchase issued by the company aren't recognized by any other organization. "They can't sell .... sun because it's not theirs to sell," states one critic of the company.

8 **What About You?** Think of an ad you've seen that you think has a suspicious claim. What is the claim, and why do you think it's suspicious?

....

....

....

....

Glossophobia, or the fear of public speaking, is believed to be the most common phobia in the world, affecting as many as 75 percent of all people.

LESSON 3

9 Complete the conversation between two friends. Use the expressions with <u>mind</u> from the box. Change verb forms and pronouns as necessary.

be all in one's mind	keep (something) in mind
be out of one's mind	make up one's mind
change one's mind	~~put (something) out of one's mind~~

Kelly: Hey, let's go to a spa on Saturday. We can relax and enjoy ourselves. Let's forget about work and *put it out of our minds* .
1.

Andrea: That sounds great, but I can't. I'm going to a class. Actually, it's a seminar—to help me get over my fear of dogs.

Kelly: Really? I didn't know you were afraid of dogs.

Andrea: Yeah. I know the reason isn't really logical or real, and the fear
_____ , but I've had trouble getting over it.
2.

Kelly: So what made you decide to try to get over your fear now?

Andrea: Well, it's a little embarrassing. People think I
_____ when I'm terrified of a tiny dog.
3.

Kelly: Everyone's afraid of something. Try to _____
4.
if you feel bad about your fear.

Andrea: I know, but it's still hard. Everyone in my family loves dogs, and they
each have at least one. So I've _____ that I want
5.
to get over my fear so I can go visit them.

Kelly: Well, good luck with the class. And if you _____
6.
about going to the spa, let me know.

10 Read the conversation again. Then check <u>true</u> or <u>false</u> for each statement.

	true	false
1. Kelly suggests visiting a spa to relieve work-related stress.	☐	☐
2. Kelly has a phobia.	☐	☐
3. Andrea thinks that her fear of dogs is irrational.	☐	☐
4. Kelly thinks Andrea's fear is crazy and foolish.	☐	☐
5. Kelly offers Andrea a suggestion to help her deal with the stress her fear causes.	☐	☐
6. Andrea has decided to try to overcome her fear.	☐	☐
7. Andrea's fear of dogs is interfering with her life.	☐	☐

11 What About You? **Answer the questions in your own way.**

1. List a few things that many people are afraid of. Why do you think people fear these things?

Common fear	Reason
bees	bee stings are painful

2. Do you know anyone who has an irrational phobia? Do you feel sympathy for that person? Why or why not?

_____

_____

3. What advice would you give to someone who wants to get over a phobia?

_____

_____

LESSON 4

12 **Read the letters to a dream interpreter and his responses.**

Ask Dr. Dream

Dear Dr. Dream,

Recently I've dreamt that all my teeth were falling out. It didn't hurt, but it was a horrible feeling. I didn't know why they were falling out, and I couldn't stop it. It was really weird and disturbing. I've had a lot of dental work done in the past, and I think my dream must reflect a fear of losing my teeth. Am I right?

**Derek B.
Banbury, England**

Dear Derek,

Losing teeth is actually a very common dream. In my experience, a dream about losing teeth is a reflection of the dreamer's concern with his or her appearance. After all, our smiles are one of the first things people notice when they meet us. In our society, we place a high value on good looks, and teeth play an important role in conveying an attractive image.

Consider how you feel about your appearance. Are you worried about what you look like? Once you accept yourself for who you are without worrying about impressing others with your looks, the dreams should stop.

Dr. Dream

Dear Dr. Dream,

I feel a little strange writing about this dream I had a few nights ago, but it's really been bugging me, so here goes. I dreamed that I was on the bus going to work when I suddenly realized that I didn't have any clothes on! I was so embarrassed! It was a really awful feeling. But the thing that was really strange about the dream was that no one else seemed to notice that I wasn't wearing anything. I'm really confused about this dream and a little worried. I'm afraid it's an indication that something bad is going to happen to me. Can you help?

**Kimberly P.
Montreal, Canada**

Dear Kimberly,

First of all, dreams are not predictions of the future, so don't worry that something bad is going to happen. My theory is that you feel vulnerable, afraid people will judge you or make fun of you. Clothes hide our bodies. Without them, we might feel like people can see who we really are. As for the fact that no one else noticed you weren't wearing anything, that's your unconscious communicating with you. It's trying to show you that your anxiety is needless. No one is going to notice or care about what you do as much as you will.

Dr. Dream

Now answer the questions, according to the information in the letters and responses.

1. What does Derek think his dream means? ....
....

2. How does Dr. Dream interpret Derek's dream? ....
....

3. Which interpretation do you agree with? Why? Or what is your own interpretation of
   Derek's dream? ....
....

4. What does Kimberly think her dream means? ....
....

5. How does Dr. Dream interpret Kimberly's dream? ....
....

6. Which interpretation do you agree with? Why? Or what is your own interpretation of
   Kimberly's dream? ....
....

13 **Complete the sentences with the correct participial adjectives. Use the present
or past participle form of the underlined verbs.**

1. Dream interpreters' ideas about dreams sometimes <u>startle</u> people.

   Their ideas can be ....*startling*......... .

   People are sometimes ......*startled*...... by dream interpreters' ideas.

2. I have a recurring dream that really <u>disturbs</u> me.

   My dream is really ....

   I am .... by that dream.

3. Nightmares can really <u>frighten</u> children and adults.

   Children and adults can be .... when they have nightmares.

   Nightmares can be .... for people of all ages.

4. Dreams can be hard to understand. Sometimes they <u>confuse</u> us.

   Dreams are sometimes ....

   People are sometimes .... by their dreams.

5. Have you ever had a dream that really <u>fascinates</u> you?

   Have you ever had a really .... dream?

   Have you ever been .... by a dream?

Grammar Booster

A Complete each sentence. Circle the correct word.

1. A **cloud / clap / gust** of smoke covered the burning building.
2. There's a **can / box / tube** of detergent for the dishwasher under the sink.
3. Would you mind picking up a **loaf / carton / liter** of bread for dinner?
4. A **clap / bolt / ray** of sunshine cut through the cloudy sky.
5. I'd like a **liter / cup / glass** of coffee with cream and sugar, please.
6. The recipe calls for one **drop / clove / bar** of garlic.
7. A **drop / bar / gust** of wind lifted the kite into the sky.

B Complete each sentence with a phrase from the box. Each word may be used more than once.

an act of	a piece of	a sense of	a state of

1. Let me give you _____ advice.
2. After the changes were implemented, many of the employees were in _____ confusion.
3. Mrs. Carson always maintains _____ control in her classroom.
4. The students' refusal to attend classes was _____ defiance.
5. After finally finishing the project, we enjoyed _____ accomplishment.
6. To do this job, it's really helpful to have _____ humor.
7. That's just _____ gossip. I wouldn't pay any attention to it.
8. After standing empty for over 20 years, the old house was in _____ disrepair.

C Complete each sentence with a word from the box. Add a if necessary. Each word may be used more than once.

fear	superstition	time	victory

1. I remember _____ when life was simpler. Things were very different then.
2. Deborah Richard's election to the presidency represents _____ for women.
3. There's evidence of interest and belief in _____ in cultures worldwide.
4. Hearing the strange noise, we all felt alarmed and looked at one other with _____ .
5. Athletes experience the joys of _____ as well as the pains of defeat.
6. According to _____ that I just recently heard, it's bad luck to walk under a ladder.
7. Neil is afraid of flying. It's _____ he's had since he was a child.
8. Do you have _____ to go get something to eat?

D **Complete the sentences with <u>a</u> or <u>the</u>. Write X if the noun should not have an article.**

1. People in different parts of _____ world have varied superstitions. For example, in some cultures _____ number 13 is considered unlucky, while in others 4 is an unlucky number, and in still others 17 is thought to be _____ bad luck.

2. Bill gave me _____ glass of water to drink. He said that _____ water at his house goes through _____ special filtering system.

3. Lucy bought _____ car last month. _____ car isn't brand new; she bought it from _____ neighbor who had driven it for less than _____ year. But it's in _____ good condition, and Lucy thinks she paid _____ fair price for it.

4. If you're in the mood for Japanese food, I know _____ good restaurant that's not too far from here. _____ restaurant just opened recently, but it's already become one of _____ most popular places in town.

5. _____ success that Jackie has had is because she's _____ hard worker. It has nothing to do with _____ luck.

6. According to _____ recent news program, _____ rich in this country are getting richer, while _____ poor are getting poorer.

Writing: Describe a fear

A Prewriting. "Freewriting" for ideas.

- Choose a fear that you have. On a separate sheet of paper, write for five to ten minutes any words, phrases, statements, or questions about the topic that come to mind.

- Consider exactly what you are afraid of, where the fear came from, how it makes you feel, how it affects your life, and how you might overcome it.

- Write quickly. Do not take time to correct spelling, punctuation, organization, etc.

- Read what you wrote. Circle ideas that go together and add more details.

B Writing. On a separate sheet of paper, describe your fear. Use your freewriting notes for ideas.

C Self-Check.

- ☐ Does every sentence have a subject and a verb? Underline all the subjects and circle all the verbs.

- ☐ Do the subjects and verbs agree? Correct errors in agreement.

WRITING MODEL

I'm afraid of upsetting other people. It's not a fear that actually causes me fright—for me it's more like I feel very nervous about doing something that someone else won't like. This fear probably stems from my childhood when my mother insisted that I always consider how my words and actions would affect other people. Now I rarely do anything without thinking about what other people will think. This fear is actually a bit annoying because it means that I feel inhibited to do a lot of things that other people do easily. For example, if I receive poor service at a restaurant, I likely won't complain because I think the waiter will get angry with me. I know in my head this doesn't make much sense, but it still feels real for me. I want to overcome my fear, and I think the way to do that is by doing things that I'm afraid of or anxious about. I think that little by little I might be able to overcome my fear.

Travel hassles and experiences

TOPIC PREVIEW

1 **Complete the chart. Compare and contrast the different types of transportation. What are the advantages and disadvantages of each? Consider the hassles that you face or can avoid with each type.**

Type of transportation	Advantages	Disadvantages
car		
plane		
train		
bus		

2 **What About You?** **Answer the questions in your own way.**

1. Which type(s) of transportation do you usually take when you travel? Why?

   ....

   ....

2. Which type(s) of transportation do you prefer? Why?

   ....

   ....

THE TEN BEST AIRPORTS IN THE WORLD*

1 Hong Kong International Airport (China)

2 Changi Airport (Singapore)

3 Seoul Inchon Airport (Korea)

4 Munich Airport (Germany)

5 Kansai International Airport (Japan)

6 Dubai International Airport (Dubai)

7 Kuala Lumpur International Airport (Malaysia)

8 Amsterdam Shiphol Airport (Netherlands)

9 Copenhagen Airport (Denmark)

10 Sydney Airport (Australia)

*Results based on a 31-question survey that asked travelers to rate issues such as wait times and service, ambience and cleanliness, ease of understanding signs, shopping and dining options, and access to public transportation.

Source: www.forbes.com

3 Read the conversation. Then answer the questions.

Leslie: What a horrendous day for traveling. I can't believe the weather. This train station is freezing!

Dave: I know. Everyone is wearing their coats. You'd think they'd get the message and turn up the heat.

Leslie: Could you hold my computer bag for a sec? I just want to find my money . . . Thanks. I'm going to get a cup of coffee.

Dave: Go for it. I'll stay here and watch your stuff.

Leslie: Thanks. Do you want something?

Dave: Um, coffee sounds good. With cream and sugar, please.

Leslie: Sure.

Dave: Wait. On second thought, I think I'd prefer tea.

Leslie: OK. I'll get you a cup of tea.

1. Does Leslie think it's a good day to travel? Why does she feel that way?

_____

2. What is "the message" that Dave refers to?

_____

3. What favor does Leslie ask of Dave?

_____

4. When Dave tells Leslie, "Go for it," what is he telling her to do?

_____

5. What favor does Leslie do for Dave?

_____

LESSON 1

4 Read each person's statements. Then complete the conditional sentences with mixed time frames. Use the correct forms of the words in parentheses. Some items may have more than one correct answer.

1. **Lindsey:** "Thank goodness I ate breakfast before we got to the bus station. There's nothing good to eat here."

   Lindsey _____*would be*_____ (be) hungry now if she _____*hadn't eaten*_____ (eat) breakfast before getting to the bus station.

2. **Gina:** "The flight was overbooked, and they asked volunteers to give up their seats. So I volunteered, and I got a free ticket to fly round trip anywhere in the country."

   If Gina _____ (give up) her seat, she _____ (have) a free ticket now.

3. **Nicole:** "It's a good thing I made our hotel reservation weeks ago. Now it's impossible to find rooms."

   Nicole _____ (be able to) find a room if she _____ (make) the hotel reservations already.

4. **Bill:** "Too bad Tricia didn't pack a few essentials in her carry-on. Now she doesn't even have a toothbrush while the airline finds her bag."

   Tricia _____ (have) her essentials if she _____ (pack) them in her carry-on.

5 Rewrite each situation as a conditional sentence with mixed time frames. Some items may have more than one correct answer.

1. I didn't check the time of the train. We missed it.

If I had checked the time of the train, we might not have missed it.

2. Jane went to the front of the security line because she's a flight attendant.

....

3. My passport got stolen, so I have to go to the embassy tomorrow.

....

4. She always worries about money. She doesn't enjoy vacations very much.

....

5. I don't have anything to read on the plane because I put my book in my checked luggage.

....

6. My brother decided to fly to Rio de Janeiro last week because he got a free ticket.

....

6 Look at the illustrations. Write sentences with mixed conditional time frames.

Two years ago

Today

1. *If she hadn't missed the train, she might not have met her husband.*

Yesterday

Today

2. ....

Earlier today

Now

3. ....

Earlier today

Now

4. ....

If you've ever lost your luggage on a trip, then you know it can be a nightmare to recover it. Despite airlines' efforts to reduce the number of lost bags, hundreds of thousands of pieces of luggage still go missing every year, a great deal of which is never reclaimed. What happens to all that stuff? Much of it is bought for a minimal price and resold by a store called the Unclaimed Baggage Center. Each year the store sells millions of items, including suitcases, clothing, cameras, and jewelry, for a fraction of their retail value.

LESSON 2

7 Put the sentences in order. Write the number on the line.

_5_ **Brian:** Thanks so much. I really appreciate it.

_2_ **Amy:** What's that?

_1_ **Brian:** Amy, could you do me a favor?

_4_ **Amy:** Of course not. I'd be happy to.

_3_ **Brian:** I've got a horrendous headache. Would you mind getting me some aspirin?

8 Write questions with either <u>Would you mind</u> or <u>Could you please</u>.

1. (move your bag out of the aisle)

   Would you mind moving your bag out of the aisle?

2. (hold my carry-on bag)

   Would you mind holding my carry-on bag?

3. (keep an eye on my laptop)

   Would you mind keeping an eye on my laptop?

4. (give me a hand with my suitcase)

   Could you please give me a hand with my suitcase

5. (let me know when the flight is announced)

   Could you please letting me know when the flight is announced

6. (get me a cup of coffee)

   Could you please get me a cup of coffe

9 Look at the pictures. Complete the questions to ask for favors. Use your own words.

1. Would you mind *turning down your music?*

2. Would you mind

3. Could you please

4. Could you please

5. Would you mind

6. Could you please

10 Write a conversation in which someone asks another person for a favor. Use one of the situations in Exercise 9 or your own situation. Use the conversation in Exercise 7 and the conversation on page 66 in the Student's Book as models.

A: ....

B: ....

A: ....

B: ....

A: ....

LESSON 3

11 Read the magazine article.

WAITING AS A WAY OF LIFE

For eighteen years, Merhan Nasseri spent every day waiting patiently on a bench in Charles de Gaulle Airport for his flight to London, suitcases stacked neatly beside him. What had begun as a travel nightmare on August 26, 1988, became a way of life. Meet the man who lived in Charles de Gaulle's Terminal One.

Nasseri's odyssey began in 1977, when he was expelled from his home country of Iran for his political views. Forced to abandon his family, Nasseri headed to Europe, where he bounced from country to country until finally, in 1981, he obtained refugee status from the United Nations. Granted the right to live in any European country, Nasseri boarded a flight to Great Britain, where he has relatives. On a stopover in Paris, however, his bag containing his identity papers was stolen. Without these documents, British immigration officials refused to allow Nasseri into Great Britain, and he was returned to France. Back at Paris's Charles de Gaulle Airport, Nasseri found himself in the ultimate travel nightmare. Without identifying documents, he could neither enter France nor travel to another nation. He had become a man without a country.

With nowhere to go, Nasseri made Terminal One his home while he waited for a decision from the French government. According to airport workers, Nasseri quickly settled into a routine. Before passengers arrived, each morning he awakened at 5:30 on the bench where he spent each night. He shaved and brushed his teeth (using toiletries from free airline travel kits) in the men's room. Careful about appearing tidy, he washed his clothing once a week in the sink and kept his belongings neatly organized in suitcases and boxes. Nasseri spent much of the day reading—keeping up with current events with the latest newspapers and magazines.

The would-be traveler was befriended by airport employees, who called him "Sir Alfred" and looked after him—donating meal vouchers, pocket money, and clothing and lifting his spirits with coffee and conversation on their breaks. He received weekly visits from the airport doctor, who worried that his confinement had affected his mental health. The subject of several documentaries and movies (most notably, Stephen Spielberg's *The Terminal*, starring Tom Hanks), Nasseri's popularity extended beyond Terminal One. He received hundreds of letters at the airport each year.

Nasseri was finally granted French residency in 1999, allowing him to leave the airport and live in France. However, Nasseri refused to leave until allowed to live in Great Britain. Friends worried that, after being confined to the terminal for so long, Nasseri might be afraid to leave. Finally in 2006, his airport wait ended when he was hospitalized for unknown reasons. He has been living in Paris ever since.

Now answer the questions, based on the information in the article.

1. Why was Merhan Nasseri originally forced to live in Charles de Gaulle airport?

   ....

2. How did Nasseri pass the time in the airport?

   ....

3. Without a job or income, how did Nasseri support himself?

   ....

4. According to the article, why did Nasseri refuse to leave the airport after he was granted French residency?

   ....

12 **What About You?** **Answer the questions in your own way.**

1. If you were in Merhan Nasseri's situation, which parts of the experience do you think would have been the most difficult for you? Why?

   ....

   ....

2. In your opinion, why do you think that Nasseri chose to stay in Terminal One in 1999 although he'd been given the opportunity to leave?

   ....

   ....

3. When Nasseri finally left the airport, what difficulties do you think he found in everyday life?

   ....

   ....

13 **Look at the pictures. What's happening? Describe the travel nightmare in each picture.**

1. ....

2. ....

3. .... **4.** ....

14 What About You? **Answer the questions in your own way.**

1. Which of the experiences in Exercise 13 would be the worst for you? Why?

....

....

2. What would happen if you went through one of the experiences in Exercise 13? On a separate sheet of paper, write a short journal entry to describe what happened.

15 Complete each sentence with the appropriate participial adjective as a noun modifier.

1. On my last vacation, my luggage was lost. When the airline was unable to locate my
.........*lost*......... luggage, they reimbursed me promptly.

2. The hotel claimed that we burned the sofa in our room with a cigarette during our stay. They
charge us a fee to repair the .... sofa.

3. A waiter spilled a glass of red wine, staining the front of my dress. I took the
.... dress to the dry cleaners, but they couldn't get the stain out.

4. My son accidentally broke a vase in a souvenir shop. Of course, we had to pay for the
.... vase.

5. A thief stole my laptop while I was eating in an outdoor café. Surprisingly, the police caught
the thief and recovered the .... laptop within 24 hours.

6. I dropped my new camera and cracked the lens. Luckily, it's still under warranty, so when I
called customer service they offered to repair or replace the .... lens.

7. Someone burglarized a suite in the hotel. The police are now searching for evidence in the
.... suite.

8. The storm was so bad that our resort had to cancel our scuba diving class. We got a refund
for the .... class, but I was really disappointed.

LESSON 4

16 Challenge. Order the pictures in your own way. Number each picture.
Then, on a separate sheet of paper, write a brief story based on the pictures
about a life-changing event. Use sequence words such as <u>first</u>, <u>then</u>, and <u>next</u>.
Add as many of your own details as you wish.

Grammar Booster

A Read each conditional sentence. Then read each pair of statements that follow.
Check <u>true</u> or <u>false</u>.

	true	false

1. If Dave were here, he'd tell us what to do.
   Dave is here. ☐ ☐
   Dave is going to tell us what to do. ☐ ☐

2. If she hadn't read the letter, she would have been shocked by the news.
   She didn't read the letter. ☐ ☐
   She wasn't shocked by the news. ☐ ☐

3. We might be on the train now if we hadn't gotten stuck in traffic.
   We're not on the train. ☐ ☐
   We got stuck in traffic. ☐ ☐

4. If I have time, I may be able to help you out.
   I am certain that I'll have time. ☐ ☐
   I will definitely help you out. ☐ ☐

5. If he had taken my advice, he wouldn't be in trouble.
   He took my advice. ☐ ☐
   He's in trouble. ☐ ☐

B Complete each statement. Circle the letter.

1. If the park gets too full, you .... wait for some people to leave before they let anyone else in.
   a. had to
   b. wouldn't have had to
   c. have to
   d. didn't have to

2. The air-conditioning automatically turns on if the temperature .... above 27 degrees Celsius.
   a. goes
   b. will go
   c. would go
   d. would have gone

3. If we had gotten the call earlier, we .... help.
   a. would
   b. will
   c. were going to
   d. might have been able to

4. Kyle studied very hard for his test. But if he ...., he would be really nervous.
   a. had studied
   b. would have studied
   c. hadn't studied
   d. doesn't study

5. I .... so excited to go to Paris tomorrow if I had been there before.
   a. wouldn't have been
   b. wouldn't be
   c. won't be
   d. hadn't been

6. If it hadn't been for the support of all the members, the team never ....
   a. would win
   b. would have won
   c. wins
   d. won

7. I .... you if you help me first.
   a. helped
   b. will help
   c. had helped
   d. would have helped

8. If it .... for that party, we never would have met.
   a. hadn't been
   b. wouldn't have been
   c. had been
   d. was

9. Heather _____ surprised right now if you hadn't told her about the party.
- **a.** is
- **b.** had been
- **c.** will be
- **d.** would be

10. If the weather _____ bad, we'll move the party inside.
- **a.** was
- **b.** had been
- **c.** were
- **d.** is

C **What About You?** **Complete the conditional sentences in your own way.**

1. If I had more free time, ...

....

2. If we arrive at English class late, ...

....

3. If I hadn't decided to ....

....

4. If I spoke English fluently, ...

....

Writing: Compare two vacation destinations

A **Prewriting. Planning ideas with a chart.**
Label each circle with one of the two places you'd like to visit for a vacation. Think about details and characteristics of each place. List information about each place under the correct name. Write similarities between the two places under BOTH.

BOTH

B **Writing.** On a separate sheet of paper, compare and contrast the two places in your chart. Use the information in your chart. Explain which place you think you'd prefer to visit for a vacation. Use expressions of comparison and contrast and conditionals.

C **Self-Check.**

☐ Did you use expressions for comparison and contrast correctly?

☐ Did you use the conditional form to describe your preferences? Did you use it correctly?

☐ Did you introduce the topic in an introductory paragraph?

☐ Did you present and support your ideas in the paragraphs that follow?

☐ Did you summarize your ideas in a concluding paragraph?

WRITING MODEL

Two places that I'd love to visit for a vacation are Nice in France and Cinque Terre in Italy. Both are very beautiful places and great vacation destinations. However, there are some differences.

Nice is a busy beach city. There are people from all over the world shopping, eating in world-class restaurants, and going to dance clubs that stay open very late. Similarly, Cinque Terre is also on the water, but the environment is very different. It is still undiscovered by many tourists. In contrast to the fast pace of Nice, most of the visitors to Cinque Terre spend their days hiking, swimming, and visiting olive groves and vineyards.

Both Nice and Cinque Terre are great for vacation. But if I had to choose just one of those places, I think I would choose Cinque Terre. For me, it'd probably be more relaxing.

Minds at work

TOPIC PREVIEW

1 Read about the employees of Ashton Corporation. Identify the kind of intelligence associated with each person's abilities. Write the letter on the line.

KINDS OF INTELLIGENCE		
a. intuitive	d. intrapersonal	g. interpersonal
b. musical	e. visual and spatial	h. physical
c. mathematical	f. linguistic	

1. .... Janice White is a genius with numbers. She can do complicated math problems in her head. She is smart with her finances, and friends often come to her for advice on money matters.

2. .... Valerie Hueso spends much of her free time painting, drawing, and creating sculpture. Some of her work was recently exhibited at a local art gallery.

3. .... Nick Richards is good at explaining things and is patient about answering questions. A born teacher, he is often asked to train new employees.

4. .... Dave Marrow works well by himself. Although a new employee, he rarely needs to ask his supervisor or other co-workers for help. He is always looking for ways to improve his job skills.

5. .... Ashley Reese is the most outgoing person in her office. She has a great sense of humor, and she always keeps her co-workers laughing. She writes poetry in three languages—her native language of English, and Japanese and Spanish—which she learned as an adult.

6. .... Vince Boyton is always one of the first to come up with new and original ways of doing things. While he sometimes makes business decisions based on his feelings rather than on facts and information, his choices usually prove to be correct.

7. .... Mac Myers has a great voice and plays the guitar very well. A few years ago he and three friends formed a band. They often perform at local events on weekends.

8. .... Debbie Tan is able to fix almost anything, which is why everyone at work turns to her when a computer, printer, or other machine breaks down. She's also really good at putting things together, especially electronics.

2 The Ashton Corporation is organizing its annual company picnic. Read the list of tasks that need to be completed. Select an employee from Exercise 1 to complete each task, according to the skills required. Give a reason for each choice.

Task	Employee	Reason for choice
1. provide musical entertainment	Mac Myers	Mac has high-level musical intelligence. His band could play at the picnic.
2. design invitations, decorations, and signs		
3. plan a budget and calculate all costs		
4. tell jokes, introduce activities		
5. set up lighting and stereo systems		
6. create a theme for the picnic and ideas for games and activities		

LESSON 1

3 Read the descriptions of the zodiac signs. Then find your sign.
Do you think your strengths and weaknesses match those described?
Explain your answer.

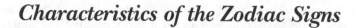

Characteristics of the Zodiac Signs

AQUARIUS (January 20–February 18) You are intelligent and inventive. With an independent (and rebellious) mind, you have your own unique way of thinking and refuse to follow the crowd. You have a talent for discovering new ways of doing things. You love electronic gadgets and figuring out how they work. Your unusual lifestyle and unpredictable nature may seem odd to some people.

PISCES (February 19–March 20) You have a vivid imagination and have a talent for writing poetry, creating art, and performing on stage. You care deeply for other people and devote time to helping those who are sick. A daydreamer, you have a habit of seeing life as you want it to be, rather than how it really is. You sometimes allow your emotions to control your behavior.

ARIES (March 21–April 19) You are adventurous and not afraid to try new things. You are always busy and never lazy. You prefer to work independently and don't have patience with people who are slower or less talented. You're not afraid to fight with others to achieve your goals. In your enthusiasm to get things done, you sometimes work too quickly and don't notice smaller points.

TAURUS (April 20–May 20) You have a fondness for luxury and relaxation. You have excellent taste in food, art, and music. After hearing a song just once, you can sing the lyrics or play the melody. Slow to act and speak, you view all sides of a situation before making decisions, and you choose your words carefully. Although some may find you too quiet, you are a loyal friend.

GEMINI (May 21–June 20) A smooth talker, you have the ability to communicate ideas clearly and persuade others to agree with your point of view. Always the life of the party, you have many friends. You are skilled at using tools and fixing machines. Your love of talk sometimes gives you the reputation of being a gossip.

CANCER (June 21–July 22) You are sensitive and emotional. Your love of family is strong, as is your need to protect and care for the people close to you. When making decisions, you have a talent for sensing the correct choice. However, you have a tendency to allow your emotions to get in the way of rational judgments. Shy and easily hurt, you are slow to make friends.

 **LEO (July 23–August 22)** You are a born leader and others naturally look to you for advice and inspiration. An independent spirit, you don't like being told what to do. You love being the center of attention and dislike being ignored. You enjoy playing sports of all kinds, especially in front of an audience. Your desire to be a star sometimes causes you to forget to be a team player.

 VIRGO (August 23–September 22) A perfectionist, you are highly critical of anything that is not done properly. You notice small things that less perceptive people miss. You pick up foreign languages easily. You are highly organized and dislike messiness. With your irresistible urge to improve everything and everyone, you are sometimes seen by others as being fussy and narrow-minded.

 LIBRA (September 23–October 22) Easygoing and charming, you get along with almost everyone. A skilled diplomat, you are good at solving problems and convincing people to compromise. You have a need for peace and avoid conflict and arguments. Because you always see both sides of any issue, you have difficulty making decisions.

 SCORPIO (October 23–November 21) Watchful and perceptive, you quickly sense other people's true thoughts or feelings. You are a good judge of people and a patient listener. However, you are intensely private, and hold back expressing your own emotions. This lack of openness prevents others from getting to know you well.

 SAGITTARIUS (November 22–December 21) Fun-loving and free-spirited, you are happiest when on the move or trying new things. You learn foreign languages easily, and your open-mindedness about other cultures makes travel a rewarding experience. A natural storyteller, you love recounting your adventures, although you often exaggerate the facts. You are easily bored.

 **CAPRICORN (December 22–January 19)** Disciplined and hardworking, you know how to get things done. Determined to succeed, you set goals for yourself and patiently take steps until you achieve them. Shy and cautious with new people, you are often uncomfortable in social situations. You prefer to work independently and have trouble asking others for help.

The head of the Vatican library, Cardinal Giuseppe Mezzofanti (1774-1849), had a real knack for languages. It's believed that when he died at the age of 75, he spoke at least 40 languages fluently. This accomplishment is particularly remarkable considering that the Cardinal never traveled outside of Italy. All his learning came from practice with visitors to the Vatican or from books.

4 Read the statements. Check <u>true</u> or <u>false</u>, according to the information presented in the zodiac descriptions in Exercise 3.

	true	false
1. Aries signs have an eye for detail.	☐	☐
2. Taurus signs have an ear for music.	☐	☐
3. Gemini and Aquarius signs tend to be mechanically inclined.	☐	☐
4. Cancer and Scorpio signs have strong interpersonal intelligence.	☐	☐
5. Leo, Libra, and Gemini signs have a way with people.	☐	☐
6. Virgo signs have a head for figures.	☐	☐
7. Sagittarius signs have strong linguistic intelligence.	☐	☐
8. Capricorn signs don't have strong intrapersonal skills.	☐	☐
9. Aquarius and Scorpio signs have a good intuitive sense.	☐	☐
10. Pisces signs have high-level abilities in visual and spatial intelligence.	☐	☐

5 Read the conversations. Write a sentence about the strengths and/or weaknesses of each person. There may be more than one correct answer.

Conversation 1
Ray: Thanks again for helping me out with those calculations today.
Diana: No problem. Glad to help.
Ray: You know, I wish I were good at numbers like you.
Diana: Do you? Actually, I'm envious of your talent for learning languages.
Ray: Really? But languages are easy to learn!
Diana: Not for me. I took four years of French and can't even make a sentence!

(Ray) *Ray doesn't have a head for figures.*

(Diana) ....

Conversation 2
Aidan: Hey, Dave. Nice job on the presentation you gave this afternoon. You got your ideas across really well.
Dave: Thanks. I appreciate that.
Aidan: I could never stand up in front of a big group and give a speech.
Dave: It's not that hard, once you get used to it. It just takes practice.
Aidan: You're probably right, but I think I'll just stick to fixing computers.
Dave: Well, you're really good at that.

(Aidan) ....

(Dave) ....

Conversation 3
Darla: Your scarf is beautiful.
Emily: Thanks. I made it myself.
Darla: You're kidding!
Emily: No. I love doing arts-and-crafts projects.
Darla: Wow, you're so talented. I love the intricate weave.
Emily: Thanks. I can't believe you noticed that. Most people wouldn't pay attention to such a minor part of the design.

(Darla) ....

(Emily) ....

Conversation 4

Andy: Ugh! This stupid watch stopped running again!

Ethan: I can take a look at it if you want. I'm pretty good at fixing things like that. Anyway, I'm sick and tired of studying. I'm never going to remember all these dates for my exam.

Andy: Why don't you make up a song to help you remember them? Put the words to a tune. That's how I usually remember things.

Ethan: That sounds like your area of expertise, not mine. I tell you what: I'll take a look at your watch, and you can help me come up with a song.

(Andy) ....

(Ethan) ....

Conversation 5

Joseph: Congratulations, Barbara. I heard you set another sales record. How do you do it?

Barbara: Honestly, I just seem to know what people want to hear, even without knowing much about them. That makes the sales pitch easy.

Joseph: You make it sound simple, but I could never be a salesperson. Convincing people to buy something just isn't one of my talents.

Barbara: Well, not everyone's a people person.

(Joseph) ....

(Barbara) ....

LESSON 2

6 Read the statements. Then complete the sentences. Circle the correct subordinating conjunctions or transition words.

1. Marta doesn't like art class. The reason is that she's not very good at drawing.

   Marta doesn't like art class **because / even though** she's not very good at drawing.

2. The only way for us to avoid getting in trouble is to finish the project tonight.

   Since / Unless we finish the project tonight, we'll get in trouble.

3. Your acceptance into college depends on how high you score on your exams.

   You'll get into college **even if / as long as** you get high scores on your exams.

4. Natalie never studies for tests, but she always gets good grades.

   Even though / Provided that Natalie never studies for tests, she always gets good grades.

5. The product is quite expensive, but many people want to buy it.

   The product is quite expensive. **Nevertheless / Consequently**, many people want to buy it.

6. Illnesses related to smoking cost insurance companies millions of dollars each year. For that reason, big discounts are given to people who don't smoke.

   Illnesses related to smoking cost insurance companies millions of dollars each year. **Therefore / Nonetheless**, big discounts are given to people who don't smoke.

7. I want that dress. I don't care if it's overpriced.

   I want that dress **even if / unless** it's overpriced.

8. Jon is a really hard worker. He wouldn't have been chosen for the job if he weren't.

   Jon is a really hard worker. **Consequently / Otherwise**, he wouldn't have been chosen for the job.

9. The company requires that you be a member of a professional association.

   You'll be hired by the company **only if / unless** you are a member of a professional association.

"It is not enough to have a good mind; the main thing is to use it well."

—René Descartes, 1596–1650, French mathematician, philosopher, and scientist

7 **Read the article.**

JOURNAL OF WORLD SCIENCE

"Intelligence" Isn't Universal

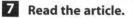

In a recent study, Ph.D.s Robert Sternberg and Elena Grigorenko of Yale University evaluated the accuracy of traditional IQ tests in measuring the intelligence of people in non-Western countries. Although these IQ tests have been successful in accurately predicting academic and career success in many Western countries, the study indicated that they may not accurately assess intelligence in other areas of the world. The study suggests that tests devised for Western cultures fail to take into account the different ways that other cultures define and reward intelligence.

The researchers used Sternberg's Triarchic Theory of Human Intelligence to assess aptitudes of children in different cultures. This model identifies three distinct types of intelligence: crystallized, practical, and creative. According to Sternberg's definitions, *crystallized intelligence* refers to academic knowledge and skills. *Practical intelligence* involves the ability to understand and deal with everyday tasks. *Creative intelligence* is a person's ability to react to new situations.

Results showed that Kenyan children who demonstrated high practical intelligence performed poorly in areas of crystallized intelligence. The researchers suggest that the reasons for this may lie in Kenyan culture. Some children are kept at home instead of being sent to school. These children, consequently, are more exposed to their indigenous culture. They learn practical skills such as identifying and using medicinal herbs. Since they do not attend school, however, they may feel uncomfortable when placed in a school environment. They score poorly on academic tests of their native language and English. Therefore, standard IQ tests which only assess crystallized intelligence may not accurately test a Kenyan child's full cognitive abilities.

Similarly, the researchers found that in Russia, a country that has recently experienced many social changes, women with high levels of practical intelligence were better able to cope with changing social conditions than other women. If a woman had strong practical abilities, she usually felt more in control of her own life despite the changes going on around her. Even if a woman scored high in crystallized intelligence, this score alone didn't predict life success in this particular culture.

Based on the results of their studies, the researchers concluded that it's dangerous to assume that the cognitive skills valued and useful in one culture are the same as those valued by another.

VOLUME 20, ISSUE 6

Now complete the chart. List the subordinating conjunctions and transitions that are used in the article.

Subordinating conjunctions	Transitions
Although	

8 Complete the sentences based on the article in Exercise 7. Use subordinating conjunctions and transitions. There may be more than one correct answer.

1. .... a person scores well in crystallized intelligence, he or she won't necessarily do well at life tasks.

2. .... researchers are careful, it's easy for them to make mistakes in measuring intelligence cross-culturally.

3. .... there are cultural differences in definitions of intelligence, it can be difficult to compare intelligence across cultures.

4. Researchers must take into consideration which intelligences a certain culture values. ...., results of their studies might be inaccurate.

5. There is no one test that can accurately measure intelligence in all cultures. ...., researchers are still interested in comparing intelligence across cultures.

9 **What About You?** Read the statements. Do you agree with the opinions expressed? Write your reaction to each statement.

1. "Even if someone scores very high on IQ and EQ tests, it doesn't prove that the person is very intelligent."

   (YOU) ....

2. "A person is intelligent only if that person has common sense. What good is being able to do math problems in your head if you're unable to function in everyday life?"

   (YOU) ....

3. "Because high IQs and EQs are crucial to success, schools and businesses should use tests to measure the intelligence of new students and employees."

   (YOU) ....

The Stanford-Binet scale is the usual standard by which IQs are measured. An average adult IQ score on this scale ranges from 85 to 115. Approximately 1 percent of the people in the world have an IQ of 135 or higher (a score indicating genius or near genius). According to estimates, which of course are an inexact science, Leonardo da Vinci had a staggering IQ of 220!

10 **Read the article.**

GET IN THE ZONE

When athletes are so focused on a task that they are unaware of any physical or mental distractions, they are said to be "in the zone." Athletes know that preparing their bodies for competition is only part of a winning formula; mental preparation is just as important. Getting in the zone means getting into your most productive state.

Corporate competition is similar in many ways to athletic competition. Performing well when the pressure's on is as important for business professionals as it is for athletes. In both fields, success depends on performing better than the competition. Focus and mental preparation are the keys to achievement.

MASTERING THESE EIGHT CONCENTRATION SKILLS WILL ENABLE YOU TO GET IN THE ZONE.

■ **Planning:** Although it's important to define long-term goals, there are a lot of steps you need to take in order to make these goals happen. The planning skill involves identifying and updating as necessary the smaller steps you need to take in order to accomplish your bigger dreams.

■ **Visualization:** Never underestimate the power of the mind. If you can imagine yourself completing a task, then you'll be successful when you're actually doing it, even if the task may be very difficult or new to you. Envision yourself working toward a goal and overcoming obstacles to achieve it.

■ **Mental preparation:** Whether it's a big sales pitch or an important presentation, you need to get your mind ready for the task ahead. Some people find it useful to review their notes right before, while others think about something completely unrelated. Find what works best for you and stick with it.

■ **Focusing:** For you to produce your best work, every bit of your energy needs to be channeled into the task at hand. You must train yourself to ignore any thoughts or outside stimuli that may distract you.

■ **Staying calm:** Anxiety and nervousness can take your concentration away from the task at hand. Techniques such as deep breathing or taking a short break can help you deal with those unpleasant feelings and get back to doing your best.

■ **Positive thinking:** Any time you're working on a task, give yourself positive support and feedback. Take time to note what you're doing well and enjoy the feelings of pride that follow. Use positive thinking to instill confidence in yourself and you can be your own biggest supporter.

■ **Boosting your energy:** There are times when you'll feel mentally and physically tired as a result of your work. Successful people learn tricks to give themselves that quick pick-me-up needed to get the job done. Next time your eyes start drooping, try eating a high-energy snack such as crackers with peanut butter or taking a brisk walk around the office.

■ **Refocusing:** Disappointment and frustration are a part of life and work, so it's inevitable that sometimes you'll experience these emotions. The trick is to recover from these setbacks quickly and redirect your full attention back to what needs to be done.

Now read about the people. For each person, choose one of the eight concentration skills in the article that you think would be most helpful to that person. Explain your answer. There may be more than one correct answer.

1. "I wish I could learn to be a better public speaker. My new job requires me to give a lot of presentations in front of large groups of people. But I'm really shy and when I get up to make my presentation, I panic. Even if I've spent hours rehearsing my speech, I get nervous and forget everything I wanted to say." — *Dave Boyle, London, England*

   The skill of staying calm would help Dave relax when he needs to make

   a presentation.

2. "I work really well in the mornings, and I usually get a lot done before lunchtime. But every afternoon at about 3:00, I feel like I'm going to fall asleep at my desk! I'm obviously not too productive when I feel like that." — *Jennifer Bowers, Wellington, New Zealand*

3. "I was recently given a task at work that I just can't see myself doing. I mean, me, overseeing an entire project? There are so many steps, and it's so involved. I can't imagine how I'm going to get it done!" — *Ana Correa de Costa, Brasilia, Brazil*

4. "I work really hard at my job, and to tell the truth, I'm pretty good at it. But I get down on myself sometimes. If things get difficult or stressful, I tend to focus on what I've done wrong or could have done better—and that just kills my self-confidence." — *Pietro di Alberto, Milan, Italy*

11 **What About You?** **Answer the questions in your own way.**

1. Describe a time when you reached your achievement zone. How did you feel?

2. Which of the eight concentration skills mentioned in the article in Exercise 10 do you think are the most effective? Which do you think are the least effective? Explain your answer.

3. Can you think of any other skills that might help people stay focused under pressure?

12 Read the article about Shakuntala Devi. Then read the statements. Check <u>true</u>, <u>false</u>, or <u>no information</u>, according to the information in the article.

A Mathematical Genius

Her name is Shakuntala Devi, but she's often known as the "human calculator." Born in Bangladore, India in 1933, Devi first astounded her uneducated parents with her calculations at just three years of age. By the time she was six, she was showing off her talents by calculating large numbers in front of university students and professors.

Having received no formal training in mathematics, Devi's abilities have stunned mathematicians. Her now-famous mental multiplication of two 13-digit numbers in 28 seconds earned her recognition in the Guinness Book of World Records in 1980. Aside from multiplication and division of very large numbers, she calculates square and cube roots as well as algorithms in her head. She took only 50 seconds to correctly determine the 23rd root of a 201-digit number. (It took a computer over a minute to complete the calculation.) If you give her any date in the last century, she can identify the day of the week within seconds.

With no formal education (in her own words, "I do not qualify to even get a typist's job"), Devi has inspired students around the world to take an interest in mathematics. "It's a myth that numbers are tough," she has said. "They are beautiful, one just has to understand them."

Devi's talents are not limited to numbers. As a child, she taught herself to read and write. She describes herself as a voracious reader. And having authored 14 books in English, she's become a prolific writer. Her books range from children's stories to mathematical puzzles to a cookbook for men.

"It's a myth that numbers are tough," she has said. "They are beautiful, one just has to understand them."

	true	false	no information
1. Shakuntala Devi has a head for figures.	☐	☐	☐
2. Devi inherited her talents from her parents.	☐	☐	☐
3. To nurture her special talents, Devi received preferential treatment at school.	☐	☐	☐
4. Devi has only average visual and spatial intelligence.	☐	☐	☐
5. Devi showed signs of genius at a very early age.	☐	☐	☐
6. Devi's intellectual genius was determined by years of formal education and training.	☐	☐	☐
7. Devi is gifted with the ability to write poetry.	☐	☐	☐

13 Challenge. **Reread the article on Sigmund Freud on page 83 in the Student's Book. Compare Sigmund Freud and Shakuntala Devi. How are they similar? How are they different? What environmental or genetic factors determined their intellectual abilities? Complete the diagram.**

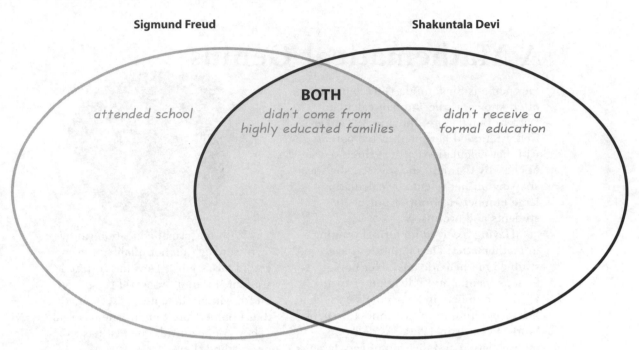

Sigmund Freud

Shakuntala Devi

attended school

BOTH
didn't come from
highly educated families

didn't receive a
formal education

Now, on a separate sheet of paper, write a short paragraph comparing Sigmund Freud and Shakuntala Devi. Describe their similarities and differences, and give your opinion on the origin of their intellectual abilities. Use the information in the diagram for ideas.

Grammar Booster

A Complete the sentences. Circle the correct word or phrase.

1. **Although / As long as / Besides** she drank coffee for over 20 years, my mother has recently switched to green tea.

2. The amount of trash produced in this country has dropped. **Otherwise / Still / In fact**, there are people who throw away things like glass, paper, and aluminum that could be recycled.

3. In my opinion, the high price of those concert tickets is worth it. **That is / Now that / Similarly**, I'd pay $100 to go if tickets were still available.

4. The best ways to lose weight are through a nutritious diet and exercise. **Nonetheless / Whereas / Unless** you change your eating and exercise habits, you'll never get results.

5. Donald Frank is an excellent candidate for the job because of his education. **While / Moreover / As a result**, he has professional experience in the field.

6. Georgia King is very generous with her time. **For instance / Consequently / Furthermore**, last week she volunteered 30 hours at the public library.

B Complete each sentence with a conjunction or transition from the box.

as long as	in other words	nonetheless	so
besides	likewise	now that	whether

1. Charlie did poorly at school but was successful in life. _____, his son James was never a good student but started a very profitable business.

2. _____ we're tested on this information or not, we should still study it. It could be very useful later on.

3. Bob Alderson really dislikes public speaking. _____, he does it frequently for his job.

4. People were stressed out for a while. _____ a decision has been made, everyone is feeling relieved.

5. Clark College appeals to a lot of non-traditional students. _____ night and weekend classes, the school offers several online courses, which allows people to continue to work while they study.

6. _____ Jean Hicks continues at her current pace, she'll easily win the race.

7. Lauren Cook has the best sales record in the company. _____, she's the company's most valuable salesperson.

8. The department head wanted to show his appreciation for the employees' efforts, _____ he took the entire group out to lunch.

C Combine each pair of sentences into one sentence. Use the conjunction or transition in parentheses and the correct punctuation.

1. Harry has only studied Italian for a year. He is the best student in the class. (however)

   Harry has only studied Italian for a year; however, he is the best student in the class.

2. Karen has a good head for numbers. She's very good at chemistry and physics. (furthermore)

   _____

3. We're facing a big challenge. We're managing to stay positive. (even though)

   _____

4. Sharon is saving money right now. She can buy a house in a few years. (so that)

   _____

5. I don't really like vegetables. I eat them because they're good for me. (though)

   _____

6. Lucia disliked the ring that her husband gave her on their anniversary. She wore it every day to avoid hurting his feelings. (yet)

   _____

Writing: Describe one of your strengths

 A **Prewriting. Brainstorming ideas.** Think about your strengths. Choose one and brainstorm ideas. Include ideas on how you got the strength (was it learned or inherited?), its effects on your life, and ways in which you might use it to your advantage in the future.

B **Writing.** On a separate sheet of paper, write about your strength, developing the ideas you came up with through brainstorming in Exercise A. Use the outline below as a guide. Be sure to include subordinating conjunctions and transitions.

> **Paragraph 1:** State the strength and summarize its effects on your life.
>
> **Paragraph 2:** Explain the strength and its effects in greater detail. Support your ideas with examples.
>
> **Paragraph 3:** Describe how your strength might help you in the future.

C **Self-Check.**

- ☐ Do your paragraphs follow the outline in Exercise B?
- ☐ Did you use subordinating conjunctions and transitions to signal causes and results?
- ☐ Did you use the correct punctuation?

WRITING MODEL

One of my strengths is my ability to communicate with others. I think I really have a way with people. Since my mom is the same way, and I never really had to work at it, I probably inherited the trait.

I think that I have a way with people because they really listen to me. For example, I was class president when I was in high school, and I was able to convince the other student leaders to change their points of view on a few issues. As a result, we made some changes to the school's policies. When I was in college, I had a part-time job at a store in a mall. I learned quickly and was able to teach other workers how to do things. Consequently, I was promoted to manager in less than a year.

My dream job definitely includes working with people. I can't imagine a job where I worked by myself all day. I'm studying right now to become a teacher. I think I'll be a good teacher because I'll be able to use my people skills to connect with students.

Humor

TOPIC PREVIEW

1 Look at the photos.

Do you find any of the photos funny? Why or why not?

_____

_____

People are more likely to laugh when they hear other people laughing. Television producers have capitalized on this fact since the 1950s by adding laugh tracks, or recordings of people laughing, to comedy programs. When we hear others laughing, we actually feel that the show is more humorous.

2 **Answer the question. Then read the article.**

How many times a day do you laugh? Do you believe that there are health benefits to laughter? What could people do to spend more time laughing?

....

....

....

Laughter Clubs Make Health a Laughing Matter

Nowadays most doctors agree that laughter provides a number of health benefits. But the challenge is to get people to start laughing.

In 1995, Dr. Madan Kataria, a physician from Mumbai, India, came up with a solution: laughter clubs. He has said that the idea for a laughter club came to him "like a divine light." People join groups for all sorts of motivation, learning, and support. Why not to laugh?

In the first few laughter club meetings, group members took turns telling jokes. But after a few weeks people had a hard time finding new jokes. Some started telling dirty and offensive jokes. So Dr. Kataria revised his idea. He decided that the club members needed to learn to laugh without any jokes or source of humor.

Dr. Kataria developed a method of self-induced laughter, which he called laughter yoga. Explaining a little about the method, he said, "In a nutshell, laughter yoga is a combination of self-induced laughter, yoga exercises, yoga breathing, and stretching exercises."

He advised, "Start with a large group —the bigger, the better." Each laughter club gathering starts with a deep-

Dr. Madan Kataria, founder of laughter yoga

breathing exercise, followed by chanting the syllables ho-ho-ha-ha-ha. Members then participate in laughter exercises, or simulated laughter. An important part of this step is for group members to make eye contact with one another. Dr. Kataria explained, "With a little bit of playfulness it becomes real laughter." And the laughter is contagious.

Most group members said that at first it felt strange to laugh for no reason. But they got used to it, and they like Dr. Kataria's methods. The laughter yoga movement has spread quickly. There are now over 5,000 laughter clubs in 40 countries around the world.

3 **Reread the article in Exercise 2. Underline three examples of direct speech and circle two examples of indirect speech. Then rewrite the sentences with direct speech as indirect speech.**

1. ....

2. ....

3. ....

A German psychologist, Dr. Michael Titze, conducted a study which showed that people today laugh less than they did 50 years ago. In his research, he found that in the 1950s people used to laugh 18 minutes a day, but today we laugh 6 minutes per day despite the huge rise in the standard of living.

4 **Read the following comments from laughter club members. Rewrite each quotation in indirect speech.**

1. One woman reported, "I've never laughed so hard in my life!"

2. A laughter yoga teacher advised me, "Let go of your inhibitions."

3. A man admitted, "I was laughing to the point of crying!"

4. A member announced, "Tomorrow we'll meet at 10:00 in the park."

5. Before his first session, he thought, "I can't make myself laugh in front of other people."

6. An experienced member warned me, "You might feel a little uncomfortable at first."

7. After her first meeting, a woman said, "I'll be here again next week."

8. Some laughter club members claim, "The group has changed our lives."

9. One doctor, who is also a club member, said, "I'm recommending laughter yoga to all my patients."

Laughing out loud for 10 to 15 minutes burns between 10 and 40 calories, depending on a person's body weight. This translates to a potential weight loss of approximately 2 kilograms a year if you do it every day.

5 Look at the comic strip. Complete the characters' conversation in your own way.

Now rewrite the characters' words as indirect speech.

1. _The boy advised the pirate that there was a storm coming._
2.
3.
4.
5.
6.

LESSON 2

6 Complete the conversation. Circle the correct words

John: Hey, I have a new joke. Here goes . . . Which animal should you never trust?
Audrey: Um, I don't know.
Natalie: Wait! Don't tell me. Um, . . . OK, I give up.
John: The cheetah!
Natalie: Ha! **That went over my head. / That's in bad taste. / What a riot!**
That joke is hilarious.
Audrey: **That's a hoot. / I don't get it. / I've heard that one.** Can you explain it?
John: The word "cheetah" sounds like "cheater." You should never trust a cheater.
Audrey: Oh. You know, **that's pretty lame / that tickled me / that's too much**.
I mean, it's really not that funny.

7 **Read the jokes. Identify the type of humor represented by each joke. Use the words from the box. Then rate each joke by checking the expression that best matches your own response.**

| an anecdote | ~~a joke~~ | a limerick | a pun | a riddle |

A man at a grocery store witnessed a woman shopping with her three-year-old daughter. In the bakery section, the little girl asked for cookies. When her mother told her, "No," she began to complain loudly. The mother simply said, "Now Monica, don't get upset. We're halfway done shopping, and soon we'll be finished."

As the mother and daughter walked by the candy aisle, the little girl asked for candy. When her mother told her she couldn't have any, the girl began to cry. The mother said, "Monica, don't cry. We're almost done shopping, and then we'll check out."

At the register, the little girl asked for gum and lost her temper when her mother refused. The mother calmly said, "Monica, we're leaving in five minutes and then you can go home and have a nice nap."

As the mother and daughter walked to their car, the man stopped to compliment the woman. "I noticed you were so patient with little Monica," he began. The mother replied, "My daughter's name is Tammy. I'm Monica."

1. _a joke_

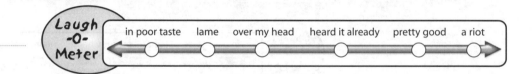

Laugh -O- Meter

in poor taste   lame   over my head   heard it already   pretty good   a riot

A small boy swallowed some coins, so his parents took him to the hospital to have them removed. After a few hours the boy's mother asked a nurse how he was doing. The nurse replied, "There's no change yet."

2. ....

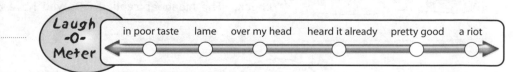

Laugh -O- Meter

in poor taste   lame   over my head   heard it already   pretty good   a riot

There once was a fellow named Tim
Whose dad never taught him to swim.
He fell off a dock
And sunk like a rock.
And that was the end of him.

3. ....

Laugh -O- Meter

in poor taste   lame   over my head   heard it already   pretty good   a riot

Breakfast Menu

EGGS
CEREAL
TOAST
COFFEE
PANCAKES

What two things can you never eat for breakfast?

Answer: lunch and dinner

4. ....

Laugh -O- Meter

in poor taste   lame   over my head   heard it already   pretty good   a riot

Tony Randall, a famous American actor, stopped in a shop one day to take a closer look at a tie he had seen in the window. The store manager was ecstatic to see the actor in his store and immediately called his wife. He dialed the phone and passed it to Mr. Randall, asking him to please say hello to her. "Otherwise, she'll never believe me!" the manager explained.

Mr. Randall was so flattered by the manager's enthusiasm that he bought the tie along with several shirts. When he went to pay for his purchases, he realized that he didn't have enough cash and asked whether the manager would accept a check. The manager replied, "Do you have any identification?"

5. ....

Laugh -O- Meter

in poor taste   lame   over my head   heard it already   pretty good   a riot

8 What About You? Answer the questions in your own way.

1. Which of the jokes in Exercise 7 do you like the best? Why?

   ....

   ....

2. Which type or types of verbal humor do you usually prefer? Why?

   ....

   ....

3. Is there any type of humor that you don't usually like? Explain your answer.

   ....

   ....

LESSON 3

"If you're too busy to laugh, you're too busy."

—Unknown

9 Read the article.

What's so funny?

Want to make people laugh? Then you've got to know what's funny. Here are a few tips to keep in mind if your goal is to tickle some funny bones.

Consider your audience.
Your audience, whether it's your kids in your living room or a paying crowd at an auditorium, must be able to connect with any situation you describe in your jokes. If they can't relate to the joke, or if they don't completely understand it, then it's simply not funny to them. People love jokes that, based on their experience, make them say, "That's so true!" If you have to explain a joke to someone, they might eventually understand it, but they probably won't think it's funny.

   This is the reason that many jokes don't translate well into another language. They rely on an understanding of a particular culture. You can translate the words but, without an appreciation for the background, many translated jokes aren't very funny.

Use surprise.
There's a reason that people say "Stop me if you've heard this one" before telling a joke. If your audience already knows (or can guess) the end of a joke before you tell it, then it's not going to make them laugh. People laugh at the end of a joke because they've been told a story and led toward its ending, (unconsciously) thinking about what will happen next or how it will end. When we hear something that wasn't what we were expecting, we find it funny.

   Surprise is part of the reason that you want to learn to tell jokes without laughing. If you laugh, then your listeners expect you to say something funny. If you tell a joke without laughing or smiling, then they're more surprised when you get to the funny part.

Check your timing.
Another important part of humor is timing, or delivering the punch line at the best possible moment. It's often useful to pause before telling the last line of a joke. The reason is that this builds tension. The listener knows the end is coming and is waiting for it. When you finally tell the punch line, the listener feels a sense of relief and is more inclined to laugh.

Now reread the article. Answer the questions, according to the information in the article. Circle the letter.

1. Which of the following is not included in the article?

   a. an explanation of why people laugh

   b. advice on how to tell a joke

   c. an anecdote about a comic experience

2. What should you keep in mind when choosing an audience for your joke?

   a. that the humor of the joke be easy for someone of any culture to understand

   b. that the audience be able to relate to the situation described in your joke

   c. that the audience be able to understand your explanation, in case they don't get the joke

3. Why do people laugh when they hear the punch line of a joke?

   a. because the ending is unexpected

   b. because they can guess the ending before you say it

   c. because you laugh and smile while telling the joke

4. What is one technique to make a punch line funnier?

   a. speak quickly before the audience can guess the ending

   b. pause before the last line, to build suspense

   c. laugh, to indicate that the funny part is coming

10 **Look at the examples of humor. If you can, explain the intended humor of each item in your own words.**

1. Why do elephants have wrinkled feet?

   Because they tie their shoelaces too tight.

   It's funny because the punch line is a surprise.
   The audience is expecting a scientific explanation,
   but instead they get the comic image of an
   elephant wearing shoes.

2. A woman walked up to a little old man rocking in a chair on his porch.

   "I couldn't help noticing how happy you look," she said. "What's your secret for a long happy life?"

   "I smoke three packs of cigarettes a day," he said. "I also drink ten cups of coffee a day, eat fatty foods, and never exercise."

   "That's amazing," the woman said. "How old are you?"

   "Twenty-six," he said.

3. ....

....

....

....

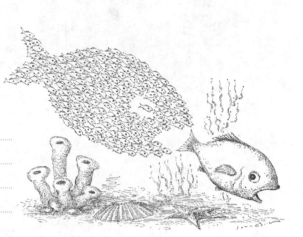

4. ....

....

....

....

Many comedians warn against analyzing humor too much.
As American author, poet, and humorist E. B. White
once said, "Analyzing humor is like dissecting a frog.
Few people are interested and the frog dies of it."

LESSON 4

11 **Read about the practical jokes. Write a sentence about each one.
Use the phrases in the box or your own words. There may be more
than one correct answer.**

cross the line	be in poor taste	be a good sport
can take a joke	be the butt of a joke	play a joke on someone

Matt asked his friend Adam to help him play a practical joke on Tricia, one of his co-workers. One day, as Matt and Tricia were waiting for their bus after work, Matt asked Tricia to keep an eye on his briefcase for a minute while he ran to a nearby newsstand to buy the paper. Then Adam came running by and "stole" the briefcase. When Matt returned, Tricia explained that someone had stolen the briefcase while she was supposedly watching it. Matt acted really angry and told Tricia that the briefcase contained something very valuable which he thought she should be responsible for replacing. Tricia refused to pay for anything.

A few minutes later, Adam returned with the briefcase and the guys explained the joke. Tricia was angry that Adam frightened her and didn't speak to Matt for a week.

1. *Adam and Matt played a joke on Tricia.* ....

Jane called a local pizza delivery place and ordered four large pizzas. She gave the name and address of her friend Mark. When the pizza was delivered to Mark's house, Mark was, of course, surprised and confused. The pizza delivery guy insisted that Mark pay for the pizzas. Finally Mark agreed, but he wasn't happy about it.

The next day Jane called her friend and admitted to sending the pizzas. Mark didn't think the joke was very funny since he'd had to pay for food that he didn't want.

2. ....

Jack glued a coin to the sidewalk near the steps of his apartment. He sat down and watched people walking by stop to try to pick it up. When they realized that the coin was glued down, most people looked around to see if anyone was watching, and they looked a little embarrassed.

3. ....

Sue chose a phone number at random out of a telephone book. Through the course of an evening she called the number every half hour and asked to speak with Brian Carr, using a different voice for each call. Each time the woman who answered the phone insisted that Sue had the wrong phone number. After several calls, the woman began to get really annoyed. A few hours later, Sue's friend Bill called the same number. He explained to the woman that his name was Brian Carr and asked if there were any messages for him.

When the woman realized the calls had been a joke, she couldn't help laughing.

4. ....

Do you find any of these practical jokes funny? Why or why not?

....

....

....

12 **What About You?** Read the quotations. Choose one and summarize its meaning in your own words. Do you agree with the point of view expressed? Explain your answer.

"It is the ability to take a joke, not make one, that proves you have a sense of humor."
—Max Eastman (American journalist and author)

"Life does not stop being funny when someone dies, any more than it stops being serious when someone laughs."
—George Bernard Shaw (Irish dramatist and literary critic)

"Humor is a rubber sword—it allows you to make a point without drawing blood."
—Mary Hirsh (American humorist, author, teacher)

"The human race has one really effective weapon, and that is laughter."
—Mark Twain (American author and humorist)

....

....

....

13 **What About You?** In your opinion, when does a joke cross the line? Write a short paragraph. Consider some of the ideas below, or use your own. Give at least one example to explain your opinion.

- if it is intended to make someone feel bad
- if it causes damage to personal property
- if the person who is the butt of the joke doesn't laugh

- if it embarrasses someone
- if it offends someone
- if someone gets hurt

Grammar Booster

A Read the conversation in direct speech. Then complete the sentences in indirect speech. Circle the correct words or phrases.

Buck: Have you heard the weather report?
Henry: It's supposed to be cold tomorrow.
Buck: Well, it'll be like every other day this week then.
Henry: Yeah, I'm tired of the cold weather.
Buck: Me, too. I can't wait for spring.

1. Buck asked if Henry **has heard / had heard** the weather report.

2. Henry said it **was / had been** supposed to be cold **the next day / that day**.

3. Buck replied that it **would be / would have been** like every other day **that week / last week**.

4. Henry said that **I am / he was** tired of the cold weather.

5. Buck agreed and said he **didn't wait / couldn't wait** for spring.

B Read the short conversations and complete the sentences in indirect speech. Then circle all the changes in nouns, pronouns, and possessives in the indirect speech sentences.

Stan: Stop me if you've heard the joke.
Will: I'll tell you if I know it.

1. Stan said ___to stop___ (him) if (Will) ___had heard___ the joke.
2. Will answered that (he) ___would tell___ (Stan) if (he) ___knew___ it.

Maya: When can I expect to receive the finished report?
Ross: Actually, it's on your desk. I left it there earlier.

3. Maya asked when she _____ to receive the finished report.

4. Ross replied that it _____ on her desk. He said he _____ it there earlier.

Kellie: What are you doing this weekend? Is anything interesting going on?
Chris: I don't know. I haven't heard about anything big.
Kellie: Well, give me a call if you want to do something.

5. Kellie asked Chris what he _____ that weekend. She asked if anything interesting
_____ on.

6. Chris said he _____. He told Kellie he _____ about anything big.

7. Kellie told Chris _____ her a call if he _____ to do something.

Angie: Will you be able to meet us for dinner?
Grace: I'm not sure. I'll have to check my schedule. I'll call you later to let you know.

8. Angie asked whether she _____ to meet them for dinner.

9. Grace replied that she _____ sure. She said she _____ to check her
schedule. She told Angie that she _____ her later to let her know.

C **Rewrite each of the following sentences in indirect speech.**

1. Jackie asked Beth, "When did you see Barbara?"

   ....

2. Seth asked me, "Can you make it to dinner on Tuesday?"

   ....

3. The teacher ordered the boy, "Put your books on your desk."

   ....

4. John promised her, "You won't be disappointed."

   ....

5. The patient admitted, "I haven't filled my prescription yet."

   ....

6. My mom told me, "Don't put too much sugar in my coffee."

   ....

7. Heather asked her sister, "Do you want to go shopping with me?"

   ....

Writing: Write a story that includes dialogue

A **Prewriting. Ordering events.** Think about a joke or story that you can tell. You don't have to choose a funny story. It can be something that you've experienced, or it can be something you've heard about, read, or seen in a movie or on television. Write a list of the main events that happened. Then make sure the events are in the correct order.

1. ....

2. ....

3. ....

4. ....

5. ....

B **Writing.** On a separate sheet of paper, write the story, telling what happened and what people said. Use a combination of direct and indirect speech. Each time you use the direct speech of a new speaker, begin a new paragraph.

C **Self-Check.**

☐ Did you use both direct and indirect speech in your story?

☐ Did you punctuate direct and indirect speech correctly?

☐ Did you make appropriate shifts in tense, pronouns, and expressions of time and place in indirect speech when needed?

What lies ahead?

TOPIC PREVIEW

1 Read the advertisements for innovative technologies. Then answer the
questions in your own way.

A.

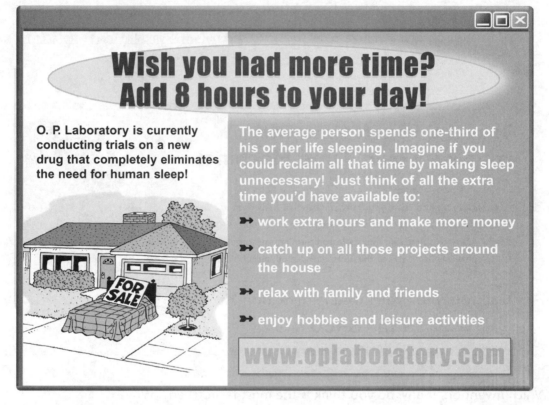

Wish you had more time?
Add 8 hours to your day!

O. P. Laboratory is currently
conducting trials on a new
drug that completely eliminates
the need for human sleep!

FOR SALE

The average person spends one-third of
his or her life sleeping. Imagine if you
could reclaim all that time by making sleep
unnecessary! Just think of all the extra
time you'd have available to:

➤ work extra hours and make more money

➤ catch up on all those projects around
   the house

➤ relax with family and friends

➤ enjoy hobbies and leisure activities

www.oplaboratory.com

B.

Under the Sea Development Company

is redefining the idea of "living space."
We're currently developing the world's first
underwater city, complete with a school
system, hospital, and a large shopping
and entertainment district.

Visit us at
www.undertheseadevelopment.com
and learn how we're giving
people a whole new idea
about the place they
call home.

CINEMA

C.

Leave the driving to us!

Himoshi Motors is about to change the way you think about driving forever.

Introducing the world's first auto-pilot car! The AutoCar is self-guided and self-driven. You just input the start and destination locations. Then the AutoCar maps out the route and actually drives you, obeying all traffic signals and relying on sensors that "see" and "hear" other vehicles and respond accordingly.

Interested in seeing the prototype for yourself? Check out www.himoshimotors/autocar.com.

D.

Travel through time with your very own Time Machine!

Just imagine being able to:

- go back in time to change the way you handled a situation
- see how your parents really acted when they were young
- give your kids a firsthand history lesson they'll never forget
- look into the future to see the consequences of your choices and decisions

Call today for your free information kit.
555-8460

1. Which invention, if any, do you think is the most far-fetched? Why?

....

....

2. Which invention, if any, do you think is not so far off? Why?

....

....

3. Which invention do you think would be most beneficial to people? Why?

....

....

4. Do you think any of these inventions might be harmful to people or society? Explain your answer.

....

....

LESSON 1

2 **Read the predictions about future technologies. Circle the passive forms.**

a robot used to find and dispose of bombs

1. According to some scientists, the need for humans to perform dangerous tasks such as firefighting (will be) (eliminated) in the not-so-distant future. These scientists predict that soon robots are going to be relied on to do jobs that could be unsafe for humans. They hope that before too long dangerous work environments will have been made a thing of the past.

an e-paper

2. In 10 years, your old print newspaper will have been replaced by an e-paper—a thin, flexible display that looks and feels like a newspaper but is entirely electronic. Forget about your morning walk to the mailbox—the news will be downloaded automatically each morning to your e-paper. The news and advertisements you receive will even be customized to match your interests and location. No need to skip through the pages of the paper that you aren't interested in!

an employee at work in a home office

3. Within 20 years, the daily commute to work will have been replaced by a short walk from the bedroom to the study. Although face-to-face meetings will still be valued, the majority of people's work will be done in offices in their own home. The need for companies to provide large amounts of office space for employees will be eliminated, and employees won't have to spend time or money to get to their workplace.

3 **What About You?** **Which of the predictions in Exercise 2 is most interesting or exciting to you? Why?**

....

....

....

4 Complete the sentences. Use the words in parentheses and the passive voice to express the future, the future as seen from the past, or the future perfect. There may be more than one correct answer.

1. Because of an increase in automated jobs, fewer people

   ..will be needed.. (need) by manufacturers in the future.

2. In 1970, a telephone that offered both sound and video was developed. Company executives confidently predicted that 3 million of these Picturephone sets .... (sell) by 1980. However, the Picturephone was a flop.

the Picturephone

3. Before the next big outbreak of disease, we hope that emergency plans .... (make) and precautions .... (take) by governments.

4. Experts now say that hydrogen fuel cells .... (accept) as an alternative source of energy within 20 years.

5. By the time the average person can travel into outer space for recreation, many trips .... (make) to all the planets in our solar system.

6. At the turn of the century, few people ever thought that in 20 years the horse .... (replace) by the automobile as the primary means of transportation.

7. In 1961, U.S. president John F. Kennedy made the bold promise that a man .... (send) to the moon before the end of the decade.

5 Rewrite the sentences. Change the underlined part of each sentence from the active to passive voice. Include a <u>by</u> phrase if necessary.

1. Within the next 50 years, <u>scientists will introduce technologies that we can't even imagine now</u>.

   Within the next 50 years, technologies that we can't even imagine now will be introduced.

2. By the year 2050, <u>people will have accepted inventions that seem incredible now</u> as a common part of life.

   ....

3. I thought <u>a secretary would answer the phone</u>, not the boss.

   ....

4. At this time tomorrow, <u>the courier will have delivered the package</u>.

   ....

5. Because of its global themes, <u>audiences all over the world are going to appreciate the film</u>.

   ....

6. After years of war, <u>government leaders will announce news of the peace treaty</u>.

   ....

6 Make predictions in the passive voice about what will or won't be done in the future. Explain your opinions. Use ideas from the box or your own ideas.

achieve world peace	increase food production
control the weather	protect the environment
discover new energy sources	provide education for all children
establish one international language	reduce costs of medication

1. *In my opinion, the costs of medication won't be reduced for a long time. Drug companies are making too much money, and they have a lot of power.*

2. ....

....

3. ....

....

4. ....

....

5. ....

....

LESSON 2

7 Put the conversation in the correct order. Write the number on the line.

.... Because it's a slippery slope. No one knows how this new technology is going to be applied.

1 You know, they say that new technologies are going to totally change the way we live our lives.

.... True. Sometimes technology develops faster than people can decide how it should be used.

.... Do you really feel that way? How come?

.... If you ask me, I think that sounds a little frightening.

8 Match each innovative technology with a possible application. Write the letter on the line.

Technology

1. .... computer chip implants
2. .... artificial intelligence
3. .... genetic engineering
4. .... cloning
5. .... remote surgery

Application

a. Saving endangered species: Genetic material taken from an animal at risk of extinction could be used to create exact copies of the animal.

b. Long-distance health care: A doctor in a hospital in New York could perform an operation on a patient who is in an operating room in Moscow.

c. Increasing food production: The genes of a plant could be manipulated in a laboratory so that it grows to three times its normal size.

d. Storing medical records: Medical workers could instantly get a patient's complete medical history just by waving an electronic device over his or her arm.

e. A car that drives itself: A built-in computer could take complete control of the car, eliminating the need for a human driver.

9 What About You? Answer the questions in your own way.

1. Choose one of the innovative technologies in Exercise 8 or another technology you know about. What are some possible applications for this technology?

Technology: ....

Applications: ....

....

....

2. What are some pros and cons to this type of technology?

Pros	Cons

3. What's your final opinion of the technology? Do the potential benefits outweigh the potential problems? Why or why not?

....

....

....

10 Complete the passive unreal conditional sentences. Use the correct forms of the words in parentheses.

1. Can you imagine having a computer chip put inside your body? According to one company that makes computer chip implants, that reality might not be too far away. The company claims that cases of identify fraud *might/would be reduced* (reduced) if implants *were used* (use) for identification.

2. At the present time, human cloning is illegal in this country. But some people argue that it should be allowed. They say that if human cloning _____ (permit), information about how certain illnesses develop _____ (learn) from cloning diseased cells.

3. If the severe side effects of the drug _____ (make) public, patients _____ (warned) about them by their doctors. But the company hid the information, causing many people unnecessary pain and suffering.

4. It seems like the possible future applications of innovative technologies are endless. For example, if the technology _____ (develop) further, computer chip implants _____ (use) instead of keys. Imagine waving your computer-chipped hand at your front door to open it instead of inserting a key to unlock it.

5. A number of soldiers were wounded in an attack far from any hospitals. If remote surgery _____ (use) to treat their injuries, many lives _____ (save).

6. Several non-governmental organizations are working to achieve equal rights for all people. The organizations' supporters say that if equal rights _____ (grant) to all people, opportunities for a new way of life _____ (create) for them.

7. In the past, consumers didn't know a lot about the dangers of certain genetically modified foods, so they were popular. If consumers _____ (inform) about the dangers, then the foods _____ (not buy).

11 Complete the passive unreal conditional statements. Use the correct forms of the words in parentheses and your own ideas.

1. If computer chip implants _____ (use) instead of credit cards, _____
_____

2. If companies _____ (allow) to clone human beings, _____
_____

3. If the Internet _____ (not / developed), _____
_____

4. If the automobile _____ (introduce) sooner, _____
_____

LESSON 3

12 Look at the graphs. Then read the statements. Check <u>true</u> or <u>false</u>, according to the information.

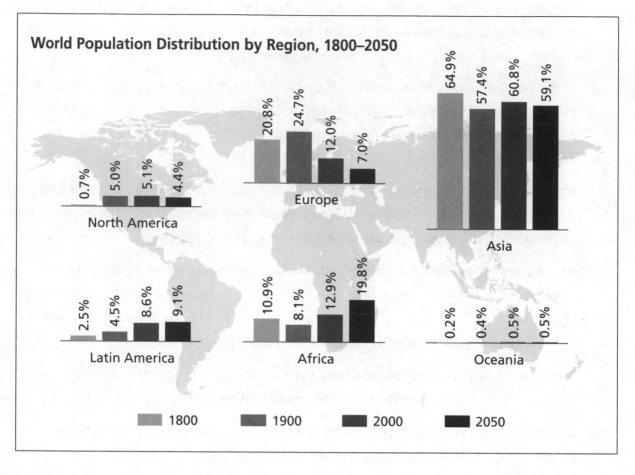

World Population Distribution by Region, 1800–2050

North America: 0.7%, 5.0%, 5.1%, 4.4%

Europe: 20.8%, 24.7%, 12.0%, 7.0%

Asia: 64.9%, 57.4%, 60.8%, 59.1%

Latin America: 2.5%, 4.5%, 8.6%, 9.1%

Africa: 10.9%, 8.1%, 12.9%, 19.8%

Oceania: 0.2%, 0.4%, 0.5%, 0.5%

■ 1800   ■ 1900   ■ 2000   ■ 2050

	true	false
1. The percentage of population increase from 2000 to 2050 is expected to be greater in Africa than the percentage of population increase in Latin America.	☐	☐
2. The largest percentage of the world's population is expected to live in Asia in 2050.	☐	☐
3. Latin America is the only region to show a consistent increase in its percentage of the world's population.	☐	☐
4. North America made the greatest increase in its percentage of the world's population in the last century.	☐	☐

13 Read the article. Then complete each statement, according to the information in the article. Circle the correct word or phrase.

Population Growth: Four Stages of Development

Population experts studying global population trends have identified four stages that nations experience as they become more developed. In the first stage, both birth and mortality rates are high, so there is little overall growth of the population. Civilization subsisted in this stage for most of human existence, moving into the next stage only within the last 300 years.

In the second stage, improvements in technology and standards of living result in decreasing mortality rates. But the birthrate at this time remains high, so there is a large population growth. Most less-developed Asian and African countries are presently in this stage.

In the third stage, birthrates decrease, resulting in a slower growth rate (if there is any growth at all) in the overall population. This is the case in several European countries, North America, Australia, and Japan, among other places.

A few developed countries, such as Germany and Italy, have now entered the fourth stage of development. In these countries, the fertility rates have dropped so low that mortality rates are actually higher than birthrates, resulting in a decline of overall population.

1. In the first stage of development, birthrates are **low / high** and mortality rates are **low / high**.

2. In the second stage of development, birthrates are **lower than / higher than / the same as** before and mortality rates are **lower / higher / the same**.

3. In the third stage of development, birthrates are **lower than / higher than / the same as** in the second stage. Mortality rates at this time are **lower than / higher than / the same as** in the second stage of development.

4. Canada is in the **first / second / third** stage of development.

5. Birthrates in Germany are **high / low**.

6. A country generally experiences its largest population growth in the **first / second / third / fourth** stage.

Today it is estimated that 4.4 people are born in the world every second. For an up-to-date estimate of the world's current population, check out www.popco.org/irc/popclocks.

14 Match the numbered vocabulary with a real-life example. Write the letter on the line.

1. .... nonrenewable resource

2. .... consumption

3. .... renewable resource

4. .... geothermal energy

5. .... pollution

a. chemicals from a factory, which leak into a nearby river

b. natural energy sources such as sunshine, wind, and moving water

c. fossil fuels such as oil, coal, and natural gas

d. heat and steam from deep inside the Earth, which can be used to heat homes

e. 83 million barrels: the amount of oil that the world uses in one day

15 Read the article.

HEVs THE WAVE OF THE FUTURE

A hybrid electric vehicle (HEV)

Most of us are aware that the cars and trucks that we drive today are powered by a resource that will eventually be used up. Oil, from which we derive gasoline, is a nonrenewable resource, and while experts disagree about how much longer world supplies of it will last, it's inevitable that eventually we'll need to find other ways to power automobiles. HEVs, or hybrid electric vehicles, provide a practical alternative to traditional gasoline-powered automobiles.

The word *hybrid* refers to something that is a mixture of two or more things. HEVs are automobiles that run on both gasoline and electricity. At low speeds with frequent stops, such as on a city street, the HEV runs on the more efficient electric motor. To save energy, the engine automatically shuts off when the vehicle comes to a stop, such as at a traffic light, and restarts when the driver puts the car in motion. At the medium or high speeds typical of highway driving, the HEV operates on its more powerful gasoline engine. The electric motor provides additional power as needed, to help the gasoline engine to increase speed or climb hills. This allows a smaller, more efficient gasoline engine to be used. As a result, HEVs use about half as much gasoline as traditional vehicles.

There are also immediate environmental benefits to driving HEVs. Electricity, unlike gasoline, is a clean energy source that does not release harmful gases into the air. Because HEVs use only half as much gasoline as traditional vehicles, they create about half as much pollution. Moreover, the electricity used by HEVs can be generated by renewable resources such as solar and geothermal energy.

If you're still not convinced that HEVs are a good option, then consider the personal advantages to buying this type of vehicle. First of all, HEVs are generally only slightly more expensive than traditional automobiles. With gas prices rising almost daily, imagine the gas in your car lasting you twice as long. You could cut your gas expenses in half. In addition, some governments offer special tax deductions to owners of HEVs.

Most major carmakers are now producing hybrid options of some of their most popular vehicle models. Based on their growing popularity, it looks like HEVs may be the next big thing in transportation technology.

Now complete the statements according to the information in the article on page 110. Circle the letter.

1. It's important that people reduce their consumption of _____.

   a. geothermal energy

   b. pollution

   c. nonrenewable resources

2. Hybrid vehicles get their power from _____.

   a. waste

   b. solar energy

   c. more than one source

3. HEVs help protect the environment because _____.

   a. they are powered by nonrenewable resources

   b. they reduce pollution

   c. they are made from recycled materials

4. Vehicles powered by both electricity and gasoline _____.

   a. don't create air pollution

   b. are more efficient

   c. are cheaper to buy than traditional cars

5. Drivers of HEVs have to fill up their gas tanks _____ drivers of traditional vehicles.

   a. more frequently than

   b. twice as often as

   c. half as often as

16 **What About You? Answer the questions in your own way.**

Would you consider buying a hybrid car? Do you think that they will become popular in your country? Why or why not?

_____

_____

_____

_____

Recycling one aluminum can saves enough energy to power a TV for three hours. There is no limit to the number of times that aluminum can be recycled. The recycling process doesn't compromise the quality of the metal, so it can be recycled again and again.

Grammar Booster

A Read the following sentences. Write <u>A</u> if the sentence is active or <u>P</u> if it is passive. Circle the passive verbs.

1. .... Laws to protect the environment must be passed by the legislature.

2. .... If the company's policy isn't working, then the managers should change it.

3. .... The president was interviewed by a famous reporter whose articles have been published in magazines around the world.

4. .... Citizens must show identification in order to vote.

5. .... The party will be attended by government officials and other dignitaries.

6. .... After years of failed attempts, the scientist finally discovered the formula.

7. .... A number of articles have been written on the topic.

8. .... First sketches of the designs are made, then samples are constructed.

B Complete each sentence. Circle the correct word or phrase in each pair.

1. My hair **had been cut / had cut** right before that picture **took / was taken**.

2. After the apples **pick / are picked**, workers **wash / are washed** them in cold water.

3. Managers **have reduced / have been reduced** prices on everything in the store.

4. A number of possible solutions **will be discussed / will discuss** at the conference.

5. Caution **should be taken / should take** when storing all household cleaners. Parents **must be kept / must keep** all hazardous materials out of children's reach.

6. The winner **will announce / will be announced** later tonight on a special two-hour program.

C Rewrite each sentence in the passive voice. Include a <u>by</u> phrase if necessary.

1. Researchers have conducted numerous studies on the topic.

....

2. First the chef chops onion, basil, and tomatoes. Then he combines all the ingredients.

....

3. Patients should take this medication with food to avoid stomach discomfort.

....

4. The judges declared Patricia Marks the winner of the country's largest singing contest. They awarded her a check for $100,000 and gave her a new car.

....

5. Passengers must provide tickets and identification before boarding.

....

6. Members of the health board, who make sure that restaurants meet state health standards, visited The Good Table Café.

....

Writing: Write an essay about life in the future

A **Prewriting. Planning ideas.**
Choose a topic and write a thesis statement.

Thesis statement:

Possible topics about life in the future:

• New technologies

• New uses for existing technologies

• Future population trends

• The environment

• Your own topic: ....

On a separate sheet of paper, make an outline to plan the body paragraphs of your essay. Write a topic sentence for each paragraph you plan to write. Follow each topic sentence with a list of supporting examples.

B **Writing.** On a separate sheet of paper, write an essay about the topic you chose in Exercise A. Follow your outline. Use your thesis statement and topic sentences. Develop your supporting examples. Don't forget to include an introduction and a conclusion. Refer to the writing model on Student's Book page 108 for an example.

C **Self-Check.**

☐ Does your thesis statement announce what the essay will be about?

☐ Does the body of the essay give sufficient support for your point of view?

☐ Does your conclusion summarize the main points of your essay and restate its thesis?

An interconnected world

TOPIC PREVIEW

1 Read each statement describing a result of globalization. In your opinion, is it a positive result, a negative result, or both? Explain your answers.

1.
> People in over 200 countries around the world drink Coca-Cola.

2.
> Much of the clothing sold in North America is made in developing countries where labor is much cheaper.

3.
> The introduction of modernized farming techniques has led to an abandonment of traditional farming methods and greater food production in some developing countries.

4.
> More and more people are learning and speaking widespread official languages such as English, French, and Spanish rather than local, indigenous languages.

2 Read the quotation about globalization. Do you agree that globalization can be both good and bad? Explain your answer and give examples.

> "Globalization is much like fire.
> Fire itself is neither good nor bad.
> Used properly, it can cook food, sterilize equipment, form iron, and heat our homes.
> Used carelessly, fire can destroy lives, towns, and forests in an instant."
>
> —Keith Porter, U.S. journalist

LESSON 1

3 Read the article. Circle the phrasal verbs.

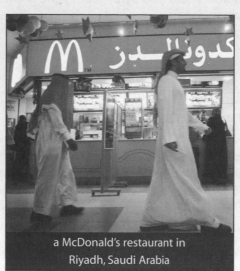

With restaurants in 119 countries, it's clear that McDonald's has become a global brand. And while there are those who criticize the company's expansion and cultural influence, others explain that individual restaurants, most of which are locally owned, modify their menus to (cater to) local diets and tastes.

Check out the menus in McDonald's restaurants around the world, and you'll likely come across a surprising number of unfamiliar choices. For example, you can pick up a McFelafel in Egypt, seaweed burgers in Japan, and rabbit in France. Enter a McDonald's in Italy, and you'll find out that you can order an espresso. Wondering about the McAloo Tikki Burger on the McDonald's menu in India? Try it out—but don't count on it including any beef. In India, you'll have to go without a McDonald's signature hamburger, as the chain's restaurants in that country don't serve beef.

a McDonald's restaurant in Riyadh, Saudi Arabia

4 **What About You?** What's your opinion of large multinational companies like McDonald's? Do you believe that they add to or take away from local cultures and traditions? Explain your answer.

....

....

....

5 Complete the conversations. Circle the correct phrase in each pair. If both phrases are correct, circle them both.

Conversation 1

Jack: This project isn't coming out the way that I imagined it at all. I think we should (**1. start it over / start over it**).

Ben: I disagree. Now that we've started, I think we need to (**2. see the project through / see through the project**). I mean, people are (**3. counting us on / counting on us**) to finish it before the deadline.

Conversation 2

Amy: We need a way to tell people about our organization.

Jason: Well, one idea is to (**4. hand out papers / hand papers out**) with our name and some information about us.

Amy: No, people just (**5. throw away papers / throw papers away**). How about pencils? We could get a bunch of pencils made with our name and website on them.

Jason: That's a good idea. Then people would be reminded of us each time they (**6. pick the pencil up / pick up the pencil**). Let's (**7. check out prices / check prices out**) for 1,000 pencils.

Conversation 3

Iris: You know, I'm really interested in (**8. taking up knitting / taking knitting up**).

Mary: Really? You should do it. But don't (**9. put it off / put off it**). Winter will be here before you know it, and it'd be great to make some hats, gloves, and scarves.

Iris: You're right. I'd better start looking for a place that offers classes. Is there any chance I can (**10. talk into you / talk you into**) taking them with me?

Mary: Actually, that sounds like fun.

Iris: All right. I'll let you know if I (**11. come anything across / come across anything**).

Mary: Sounds good.

Hooray for . . . Bollywood?

The most popular films in the world do not actually come from Hollywood. Although films from the United States remain very popular worldwide, the Indian filmmaking industry, known as Bollywood, now serves as the primary source of entertainment for more than half of the world's population. While Hollywood releases an average of 450 movies per year, Bollywood is putting out almost three times as many: 1,200 movies per year. According to one BBC poll, the most famous actor in the world isn't an American film star, but Bollywood legend Amitabh Bachchan.

**Indian film star
Amitabh Bachchan**

LESSON 2

6 Complete each paragraph. Circle the correct phrasal verb in each pair.

1. Based on the following fact, many people say that it's time to **bring about / put up with** changes in global education: It would cost $8 billion to provide basic education to every child in the world. There's no reason why any child should have to **go without / lay off** an education.

2. Scientists now say that rising ocean temperatures due to global warming will **carry out / wipe out** plankton, the microscopic plants upon which the ocean's food chains are based. If plans are not **put up with / carried out** to stop global warming, all marine life is at risk of extinction.

3. Cholera is an infection of the large intestine. When a person **comes down with / comes up with** the disease, the results can include rapid dehydration and even death. The current cholera epidemic in Africa has lasted for more than 30 years.

4. In the past several years, factory workers in this country have had to **put up with / bring about** declining wages, higher costs for medical benefits, and longer working hours. Now these workers face a new challenge—companies are **carrying out / laying off** employees and moving their factories to less–developed countries where labor is much cheaper.

7 Complete the chart. Make a list of issues that affect the world today. Identify possible problems that these issues could create, and suggest possible solutions. Then answer the questions.

World issues	Possible negative results	Possible solutions
global warming	rising ocean temperatures wipe out marine life	come up with new energy sources to replace those that cause global warming

1. What global issues are you most concerned about? Why?

   ....

   ....

2. What global issues are you least concerned about? Why?

   ....

   ....

LESSON 3

8 Complete the sentences with the words and phrases from the box.

employment rate	import	investment	unemployment rate
export	income	standard of living	wages

1. The Swedish people enjoy a high .... Sweden is among the top 10 richest countries in the world. Literacy rates are close to 100 percent and the life expectancy is high.

2. Brazil is the world's largest producer of coffee, which is an important .... for the country.

3. When Babacar first moved to Dakar, he got work in a grocery store earning .... of less than $1 per day. Through hard work, Babacar saved enough money to open his own business. His yearly .... is now more than $100,000 per year.

4. As new businesses open and hire more workers, the .... of the city goes up.

5. Mr. Edwards put some of his savings into a very small company over 20 years ago. Since that time, the company has become very successful, and Mr. Edwards's .... has made him a lot of money.

6. Like many countries, Greece depends heavily on oil from other countries. In fact, oil is the country's largest ....

7. When a country's .... starts to rise, it's usually a sign of a weak economy.

Sweatshops

The Price of Development?

A typical Western response to sweatshops has been to boycott, or refuse to buy, any imports made under these conditions. Surprisingly, however, opinion polls show that most people in developing countries view these sweatshop jobs positively. Although sweatshop workers in developing nations hope for better wages and working conditions, they don't want consumers in developed nations to protest the situation by refusing to buy the products they make. These boycotts could lead to the closing of factories and employees losing their jobs. Many workers feel that working under these conditions is better than having no job at all.

One of the most publicized results of globalization in recent years has been the transfer of well-paid manufacturing jobs from developed countries to less-developed ones, where workers can be paid much less and goods are significantly cheaper to produce.

Critics of this trend have been vocal. In the developed countries where manufacturing jobs are disappearing, labor protesters claim that the resulting rise in the unemployment rate is hurting the national economy. Critics also point out that when the jobs move to developing countries, the working conditions at many facilities in developing countries are far below the accepted standards in developed countries. At these facilities, commonly known as "sweatshops," employees work long hours, often in dangerous conditions, for low pay. Without government laws against child labor, some workers are as young as five years old.

Moreover, some experts point to statistics showing that sweatshop labor has had a positive economic impact on some developing countries. Average incomes for sweatshop workers are now 5 times what they were less than 20 years ago. The working conditions at some factories have improved, as each company tries to attract the best workers. Decreasing infant mortality rates and rising levels of education are indications of an increased standard of living.

While the pros and cons of sweatshop labor continue to be debated, one fact remains clear—the world economy is rapidly changing into one free-flowing global market. The challenge will be to come up with a way to make globalization work for the benefit of everyone.

Now read each statement. Check <u>true</u> or <u>false</u>, according to the information in the article.

		true	false
1.	The article describes workers moving from developing countries to developed countries in search of jobs.	☐	☐
2.	The number of manufacturing jobs in developed countries is rising.	☐	☐
3.	Factories with poor working conditions are known as "sweatshops."	☐	☐
4.	The article presents arguments both for and against sweatshop labor.	☐	☐
5.	Products that are made by low-paid workers are commonly known as "imports."	☐	☐
6.	Some workers in developing countries have decided to stop buying products made in sweatshops.	☐	☐
7.	Statistics show that wages for sweatshop workers in some countries are rising.	☐	☐
8.	Statistics suggest that sweatshop jobs have increased the level of wealth and comfort in some developing countries.	☐	☐
9.	The article recommends that the globalization of the world economy be stopped.	☐	☐

10 **What About You?** Do you know where the things you buy are made? Look at the labels of some things you own. List each item and its country of origin below. Then answer the questions.

Item	Country of origin

1. Do you think it's important to buy products that are made in your own country, rather than to buy goods imported from other countries? Explain your answer.

   ....

   ....

   ....

2. Do you think that boycotts are effective at changing bad company practices? Have you ever participated in a product boycott yourself?

   ....

   ....

   ....

LESSON 4

11 Read the people's opinions on language and international communication.
Then answer the questions in your own way.

1. "I don't see why we need to have an 'international' language. That's what translators are for."
— *Menes Beshay, Egypt*

2. "I think an international language is a good idea, but I think it should be a created language, like Esperanto, so that no one has the advantage of it being their native tongue." — *Callia Xenos, Greece*

3. "Sure, it makes sense to have an international language, but why not make it something other than English? I mean, Mandarin Chinese has nearly three times as many native speakers as English. Why don't we learn that instead?"
— *Alfredo Vivas, Chile*

4. "English is the best choice for an international language because it's already been established as the language of business and science. More websites are in English than in any other language, and it's the most popular second language in the world to learn." — *Donat Gorzowski, Poland*

1. Which of the opinions above most closely matches your own?

....

2. Do you think an international language is a good idea? Why or why not?

....

....

3. In your opinion, is English a good choice for an international language? Why or why not?

....

....

12 **Read the dictionary definitions. Then use the key to answer the questions.**

com·pe·tence /ˈkɑmpətəns/ also **com·pe·ten·cy** /-pətənsi/ *n.* **1** [U] the ability and skill to do what is needed: *Players are judged by their competence on the field.* **2** [U] a special area of knowledge: *It is not **within my competence** to make such judgments.* **3** [C] FORMAL a skill needed to do a particular job—compare INCOMPETENCE

he·gem·o·ny /hɪˈdʒɛməni, -ˈgɛ-, ˈhɛdʒə,mouni/ *n.* [U] a situation in which one state or country controls others

in·dig·e·nous /ɪnˈdɪdʒənəs/ *adj.* **1** indigenous people, customs, cultures, etc. are the people, customs etc. that have always been in a place, before other people or customs arrived **2** indigenous animals, plants, etc. have always lived or grown naturally in the place where they are, as opposed to others that were brought there: [+ to] *Red foxes are indigenous to the East and Midwest parts of the U.S.*

lin·gua fran·ca /ˌlɪŋgwə ˈfræŋkə/ *n.* [C] a language used between people whose main languages are different: *Swahili is the lingua franca of East Africa.*

prom·i·nence /ˈprɑmənəns/ *n.* **1** [U] the fact of being important and well known: *The case **gained prominence** (=became well known) because of the brutal nature of the murders.* | **come/rise to prominence** *Brubeck rose to prominence as a jazz pianist in the 1950s.* **2** [C] FORMAL a part or place that is higher or larger than what is around it

KEY		
Grammar Codes		
[C] countable	**Parts of Speech**	
[U] uncountable	*adj.*	adjective
[I] intransitive	*adv.*	adverb
[T] transitive	*n.*	noun
[I,T] intransitive or transitive	*v.*	verb

Excerpted from *Longman Advanced American Dictionary* © 2005

1. Which three words have multiple meanings? ....

2. How many of the dictionary words are nouns? ....

3. Which entry contains an antonym (opposite)? ....

4. Which two words can be both countable and uncountable? ....

Esperanto is a created language, constructed in the 1870s – 1880s by Dr. Ludovic Lazarus Zamenhof of Poland. Zamenhof wanted to come up with a new language that was relatively easy to learn. He hoped that the language would be used internationally as a tool for communication and that it would help to promote global peace and understanding. Although Esperanto has no official status in any country, there are currently 2 million speakers of the language around the world.

Seeking a global language

Due to its far-reaching effects and **prominence** in many parts of the globe, English is now commonly referred to as an international or global language. It is an official language in 52 countries and has **lingua franca** status in many others. It is the most widely learned foreign language worldwide. It has been estimated that between 20 and 33 percent of the world's population understand and speak English with some level of **competence**. It has become the most useful language to learn for international travel and business. It is the official language for aircraft and airport communication and is often the chosen language of international diplomacy.

Arguments have been made for and against the adoption of English as a global language. Proponents point out that a global language can lead to better international communication and an easier exchange of information (for example, on the Internet). On the other hand, the existence of one global language can increase the divide between those who know it (often better-educated people) and those who don't. There is also some concern that as English is used more and more globally, it might lead to a cultural **hegemony** of countries where English is spoken as a native language. An additional concern about the spread of English is that **indigenous** languages spoken by smaller groups of people may die out. Of course, some of these arguments would be true for any global language (except for a created one), not just English.

Now read each statement. Check <u>true</u> or <u>false</u>, according to the information in the article.

	true	false
1. The main topic of the article is a discussion of the pros and cons of learning foreign languages.	☐	☐
2. English is often described as a global language because it is so well known throughout the world.	☐	☐
3. English is often used between two people whose first language is not English—for example, a French person speaking to a Chinese person.	☐	☐
4. One argument against using English as a global language is that it's very difficult to learn—very few people achieve a high level of competence.	☐	☐
5. Some people are concerned that the use of English as a global language would give English-speaking countries too much power.	☐	☐
6. There is a concern that if English is adopted as a global language, people may stop using less common local languages.	☐	☐
7. The article concludes that English is the best choice for a global language.	☐	☐

Grammar Booster

A Underline the phrasal verbs in each sentence. Then write <u>T</u> if the sentence has a transitive meaning or <u>I</u> if it has an intransitive meaning.

1. .... It's a formal event, so everyone should dress up.

2. .... After hearing the news, the committee called off the celebration.

3. .... When I think back on those times, they seem like so long ago.

4. .... The girl grew up in a small fishing village in the north.

5. .... It's incredibly rude to cut someone off when they're speaking.

6. .... Please look your essay over before you send it to your teacher.

7. .... He agreed to go along with the story, but he wasn't happy about it.

8. .... Please, sit down and make yourself comfortable.

9. .... The conference was a little boring, but we came away with some good information.

B Read each sentence. Write <u>T</u> if the sentence has a transitive meaning or <u>I</u> if it has an intransitive meaning. Then match each definition to the way the phrasal verb is used in each sentence.

1. _I_ You're being ridiculous. Stop carrying on like that!   continue

2. _T_ We've carried on many of the traditions from when we were children.   behave in a silly way

3. .... We blew up balloons to decorate the room for the party.   suddenly become very angry

4. .... A devoted Tigers fan, John blew up when he heard they had lost the game.   fill with air

5. .... I don't want to fight anymore. Let's make up.   end an argument

6. .... My grandfather used to make up stories that even the adults loved to hear.   create

7. .... Can you turn up the volume on the TV? I can't hear it.   appear

8. .... After looking everywhere for my keys, they finally turned up under the couch.   raise, increase

C Underline the phrasal verbs in each sentence. Then write <u>A</u> if the sentence is active or <u>P</u> if it is passive.

1. .... The memo was thrown out because we thought it was trash.

2. .... Someone used up all the hot water before I could take a shower.

3. .... The poster had to be done over again because the first one was a disaster.

4. .... They passed out coupons and prizes at the door.

5. .... That group of kids always leaves Ginny out when they play games.

6. .... The passengers on the bus were let off at the corner.

7. .... The application had been filled out with a blue pen.

Writing: Write a letter to the editor

Writing a letter to the editor of a newspaper or magazine is one way to express your opinion on issues that concern you. Many publications regularly include a special section for letters they receive from their readers.

A **Prewriting. Generating ideas.**

- Choose a controversial issue in your city or country that you're concerned about. For ideas, consider current news topics, governmental laws and policies, or social, cultural, and economic issues.

- List what you think are some of the pros and cons related to this issue. Then think about your own point of view.

Issue: ....

Pros: ....

....

Cons: ....

....

....

Example:

Issue: *Raising taxes for the wealthy*

Pros: *The wealthy can affor to pay more.*

Government services may not continue without

more tax revenues.

Cons: *Wealthy business people will make fewer investments,*

and that's bad for the economy.

It isn't fair to make only one segment of society pay more.

B **Writing.** Choose a newspaper or magazine to which you'd like to write a "letter to the editor." On a separate sheet of paper, write a formal letter expressing your point of view. Acknowledge other points of view and support your own with information, facts, examples, and explanations. Then summarize your main points. (If you'd like to write a real letter, a publication's specific instructions for submitting a letter to the editor are usually at the bottom of the publication's page where the letters appear.)

C **Self-Check.**

☐ Do you express your point of view clearly?

☐ Do you include opposing arguments?

☐ Do the body paragraphs of your letter make persuasive arguments to support your point of view?

☐ Does the concluding paragraph summarize your point of view clearly?